I0054533

Dollars

AND

Sense

Dollars
AND
Sense

A WOMAN'S GUIDE TO
HOMEOWNERSHIP AND
FINANCIAL EMPOWERMENT

Megan Ethier

BURMAN BOOKS
MEDIA CORP.

BURMAN BOOKS
MEDIA CORP.

Published 2024 by Gildan Media LLC, aka G&D Media
by arrangement with Burman Books Media Corp.
www.GandDmedia.com

DOLLARS AND SENSE. Copyright © 2024 by Megan Ethier and
Burman Books Media Corp. All rights reserved.

No part of this book may be used, reproduced or transmitted in any
manner whatsoever, by any means (electronic, photocopying, record-
ing, or otherwise), without the prior written permission of the author,
except in the case of brief quotations embodied in critical articles and
reviews. No liability is assumed with respect to the use of the information contained within. Although every precaution has been taken, the
author and publisher assume no liability for errors or omissions. Neither is any liability assumed for damages resulting from the use of the
information contained herein.

Edited by Lara Petersen
Book Design by Clarissa D'Costa

Library of Congress Cataloging-in-Publication Data is available upon
request

ISBN: 978-1-7225-9906-5

10   9   8   7   6   5   4   3   2   1

TABLE OF CONTENTS

CHAPTER 1
HISTORY

Home ownership or building wealth in any true sense of the word seems unrealistic for many millennials. I get it, I am one. I've read all the articles about how millennials are lazy and don't know the value of a dollar, and if we would just stop buying avocado toast, our financial woes would wane. The truth is, millennials work more hours and more jobs than any previous generation, yet we are not climbing the societal ladder for our efforts.

Millennial women, especially, are killing themselves to remain stagnant in their pursuit of wealth. Their upbringing was marked by confusion because they were raised in homes with traditional gender roles, yet they were encouraged to harness independence. In theory, millennials were taught that they could have it all, but they had no foundation for what that looked like or what having it all really meant. The young men who partnered with millennial woman and fathered their children were also raised in homes that cultivated traditional gender roles. There was an unspoken assumption that they would be financially independent simply because that's the way it had always been.

Now that millennials have entered adulthood, the deafening silence that young boys grew up with has become the voice screaming in their heads. The un-had conversations about participating in their home life, instead of just showing up for it, are now affecting the bonds of society. A few uncomfortable truths have now entered the chat:

1. Men are less financially independent than every generation that came before them.
2. Women often earn more than their partners and work a lot harder to achieve the same fruits as their partners' labors.

Let's start with a bit of history. For centuries, women could not own property. In fact, women *were* property—a commodity men could barter for and trade. Their value to society resided in the ability to procreate and carry out the menial tasks of ensuring the continued evolution of the human race. And they were expected to do it with a smile. Little by little, women scratched, clawed, and marched their way to securing greater rights.

Our grandmothers rolled up their sleeves and flooded the workforce in droves during World War II with our girl Rosie the Riveter leading the charge. Rosie asked, "Can we do it?" and the chant that reverberated across the nation was a proud and unanimous, "Yes, we can!" And they did it without question. Women saw a need and they filled it because, if not them, then who? A common theme that remains relevant today is that women silently fill in the gaps, and often without question. When shit hits the fan or something needs to be done, there is an overwhelming, albeit silent assumption that women will figure it out, and they always do.

In the seventies, mothers burned their bras as the second wave of feminism rolled across North America. That act of rebellion granted them their rights to bodily autonomy, won them the ability to get credit cards in their own names, and to buy property. Upon reflecting on women's progress over the last one hundred years, the missing common denominator has always been men. They make up fifty percent of society, but what role did they play in the movement and pursuit of equal rights?

Many men recognized the importance of women having human rights and fought alongside them. They even graciously showed up for the topless protests, in the name of equality, of course. At the time, all levels of government were held by men, and they eventually granted women their rights. While some may argue that this was a major breakthrough for men, it should not be forgotten that we're talking about the same government that denied women their rights in the first place. You don't get to start the fire *and* receive credit for putting it out. Society has done a wonderful job of gaslighting women to make them feel excited and even thankful for the men who, crumb by crumb, granted them basic rights. Women were taught to fear the witches instead of the ones who burned them at the stake.

By the twenty-first century, gender equality had been established, affording women and men the same rights under the law. There are no legal barriers that prevent women from being as financially successful as men. However, as a working woman and a working mother, the societal barriers are crippling. My favorite part about the term *working mother* is that there is no equivalent term used as flippantly for a working father. He is simply a father. There has never been a question as to whether he worked or not. Of course a father works. He has a family to provide for! A man must have a job because that is the expectation and the societal norm.

In the last century, women's lives and places in society have dramatically shifted. The glass ceiling in the workplace has been shattered. Although women have made strides in the workplace and have achieved some level of equality, they continue to face challenges because of the traditional gender roles and expectations placed on men. These societal expectations include stereotypes related to caregiving, leadership roles, or traditional gender norms, which can limit opportunities for women to advance or be seen as equal to men.

Young women today are formally educated, intelligent, and, in theory, empowered. The echoes of their foremothers who chanted "yes, we can," in combination with the weight of their plight that rests on the shoulders of today's young women, means they are the first generation in history deemed to truly have it all. Today's young women have thriving careers and beautiful babies at home. But is this truly what our foremothers wanted for them?

Millennial women are bringing home the bacon and frying it up, and they're doing it while running carpool, planning birthday parties, researching developmental milestones and safe-sleep practices, and prepping for the PTA bake sale. And don't you dare show up without sugar-free, gluten-free, egg-free, nut-free, and vegan options. If you do, you will inevitably bear the stare of shame from Karen as you feed your child a regular damn cookie, because don't you know that will irrevocably hinder their development?

Today's women are doing it all because, after so graciously being granted the ability to join the workforce, the expectation that they will not neglect their homemaking responsibilities is still in place. Once again, women are being forced to prove themselves. They have to prove that they are worthy of working outside of the home and that they can keep up with the unpaid domestic labor. This expectation and the mentality of women doing it all has been slow to change. Women are called superheroes and rock stars, as if this somehow makes up for a lack of actual physical support and equal opportunity. Men have no issue with women contributing 50/50 financially, but god forbid they set their smartphones down long enough to fold a load of children's laundry. Equality exists in law alone, but the division of labor is far from balanced.

Over the past several decades, society has made great strides in closing the gender pay gap. Within that time, women proved to be contributing members of the working class. In most positions, they can be just as effective, if not more effective, than men with the same job responsibilities. Often, the primary argument for the discrepancy in pay is now that women work fewer hours, take more time off, and choose traditionally lower paying professions than men.

On the surface level, this may seem true; however, historically, men held all positions and wages of certain professions gradually dropped as women took them over. Two popular fields of work that women choose (and have historically been made available to women) are nursing and teaching. These professions were regarded as an extension of their primary responsibilities of caregiving and child-rearing, making the transition from home life into the workforce appear effortless.

It's no coincidence that health care and education are also the two most scrutinized fields, trashed in the media for demanding fair wages, safe working conditions, and respect. The negotiations for contract renewals make headlines upon every renewal. I have yet to see the same polarizing front page news when it comes to doctors or police departments.

Women also often choose their field of work to meet workload requirements outside the home. Mothers take more time off work than fathers because they are most often the first parent that daycare operators call when the kids are sick. Mothers are the ones who are scheduling and going to children's check-ups and other appointments. They are the ones who are up all night when the children are sick, which makes women more susceptible to illnesses that require them to take time off work for their own wellbeing.

The reason women take more time off work than men is convoluted and not as black and white as the common belief that men work harder. Women provide men with the opportunity to work more because mothers shoulder the unpaid labor of child-rearing. Teachers have hours that meet their children's needs and negate the need for outsourcing childcare. In contrast to private-sector employment, jobs in healthcare and education are typically unionized, where wages are non-negotiable and raises are not based on performance.

If women are feeling overwhelmed with their domestic workload, conversations are always framed in the lens of the women needing help. "It's so nice you have a husband who helps with the kids," or "You're lucky that your husband helps with dinner."

Am I? Am I *really* lucky that my husband performs the menial task and legal obligation of throwing some plain macaroni noodles and sliced strawberries on my toddler's plate for dinner? Don't forget the ketchup to dip!

These types of comments make me white hot with rage for a couple of reasons. First, using the word "help" indicates that, by default, domestic labor is a woman's job and her partner is going above and beyond to contribute to her workload where she is perceived to be falling short. Second, these actions should not be praised as the gold pillar of adulting. These are basic tasks that contribute to the children's wellbeing and the upkeep of the home. These are the children he took part in creating (without complaint) and the home he lives in. The bar is on the floor.

When my parents' generation see me in the store packing groceries between my baby in the bucket seat and my toddler in the front of the cart, all while hearing "Cleanup in aisle five!" because my three-year-old insisted on holding the giant tub of yogurt, I will get comments like, "Your baby is so cute," or "Helping Mom with the shopping today?" Of course, it's lovely and well natured, but when my husband does the exact same task, older women grasp their pearls and roll out the red carpet for the Father of the Year.

When a dad performs a menial daily task, such as providing food for his family, it's a pillar of excellence. When a mom does it, it's an expected and overlooked task. Even if Dad is doing the actual shopping, I guarantee Mom is the one keeping the mental list of what is needed. How much baby formula is left? Do we need to bring a treat for the Halloween party at daycare?

The mom provides the shopping list and continues to bear the mental load of remembering what goes on it. When the groceries come home, often the mom is the one who will clean the fridge and then unpack, sort, and put everything away. Even if the men in the home are contributing equally, society still views their contributions as more important than women's. When women feel overwhelmed or like they're drowning in domestic labor, the work gets outsourced to other women. They hire babysitters and cleaners, and outsource home-cooked meals. The cycle continues.

Historically, the narrative has been that men need to work long hours to support their families, and that was their sole responsibility. At home, their job is to perform the occasional oil change, mow the lawn, and open that damned jar of pickles. Women have been conditioned to accept the narrative that men's careers take precedence because they need them to. Men put in a hard day at the office and women never knew any differently because they never worked in an office. Little did women know that men's hard days consisted of pounding Tom Collinses and their secretaries during their lunch breaks.

Spending more hours outside the home does not equate to more hours worked, and this bullshit ends now. Women do not need men to provide for them financially. The opportunity for women to provide for themselves was always strategically kept from them. Men have had the opportunity to excel in their fields of choice because of women. Men have always built their careers and their wealth on the backs of unpaid labor of women.

Let's break down a normal day in the life of my family as an example:

My husband wakes up around 6 A.M. each morning, has a shower, kisses the kids and I goodbye, hops in his truck, and then grabs a hot cup of coffee to enjoy on his way to work. I also wake up around 6 A.M., but after being up three times during the night to take care of the baby. The toddler had an accident, so I give him a quick bath and get him into a clean pair of pajamas. I strip his bed and start the laundry, and then the baby wakes up. That means another diaper change and a morning nursing. I let the dog outside and then I feed it. Now it's time for breakfast. I get something for the toddler and get him organized at the table. I then get the baby in the highchair and start feeding her some mushed-up food *du jour*. Once breakfast is done, everyone needs to be cleaned up and the floors need to be swept because eating with a toddler and baby is akin to dining with the Tasmanian devil himself. I put the dishes leftover from the night before and from the morning into the dishwasher and get it started. I get the toddler dressed and his bag packed with extra clothes, a clean blankie, and a water bottle. I get the baby dressed and then flip the bedding from the washer to the dryer. Then, with my last ounce of motivation, I get myself ready for the day. A morning shower is a luxury long gone, so I get myself dressed and run a brush through my hair and we're out the door. I get both kids buckled into car seats and we're off to daycare. Once we're there, everyone gets unbuckled and inside, and after a quick kiss and a squeeze, the toddler is off for the day. I head back out and get the baby loaded in the car again, and we head to the office. When we get there, I get her out of her car seat and into a little baby bouncer I keep there. I make a coffee, open my laptop, and pull up my emails. Once I get the baby out of the bouncer and settle in to nurse again as I read my morning emails, and only then can I enjoy my morning coffee.

The discrepancy between our morning routines is stark. Was this a joint decision? Yes. Was this what we both felt was the best decision for our family? Also yes. Is it equal? Absolutely not. This is not an attack on my husband, but a way of putting the spotlight on the division of labor. This cannot be overlooked. My husband had an opportunity to excel at his career, unabated by domestic responsibilities. I support him by carrying the unpaid and overlooked labor of child-rearing and homemaking.

I draw attention to the inequality simply to make this next point. Despite these barriers to work, and barriers to wealth, many women are becoming more independently wealthy than ever before. Women are nothing if not determined and exhausted.

I was born in 1988 and grew up in the nineties in a household with traditional gender roles. My dad owned his own business and worked long hours outside the home. He was the primary financial provider for the family. From a young age, I was very well aware that his career was far more important than my mother's. My mom worked a part-time job in the public school system and took on the entirety of the domestic labor. Looking back now, as an adult with two young children, I have to assume there was a time in my parents' lives that mirrored my present life. My mom would get up with my sister and me, get us fed and dressed, pack our bags, and get us out the door to daycare or school before she began her own workday. In the evening, it was the reverse. My dad would hang out on the couch with a beer after his day to unwind while she was still in the kitchen scrubbing dishes. She would even tell us kids, "Don't bother your father, he's had a long day," even though she was still working, and he was just chilling with a drink. Yes, the patriarchy was alive and well in our home.

If you are anything like me, the thought of buying your first home didn't cross your mind until after you had your first serious partner. As a woman, it never occurred to me that I could buy property independently, or that I could independently generate wealth. In theory, I was aware that women could legally do such a thing, but none of my personal experiences provided examples of how this could be done. Among the families I know of my parents' generation, if the women worked at all, they mostly held part-time jobs. If they worked full time, it was clear that their careers played second fiddle to the patriarchs.

I always wanted to be an entrepreneur with the ability to earn an income uncapped by wage scales or seniority promotions. When I was in my late teens and young twenties, I discussed the ideas I was excited about with my family. They talked me out of every single one. They said I needed to go to university and then get a job. This was the only accepted path forward. A job looked good on paper and that was the expectation. I needed to work for someone else who would provide me with a paycheck in exchange for showing up every day.

So, what did I do? I went to university for general arts and took a couple of philosophy classes. My parents were thrilled! They got to tell their friends that their daughter was a university student and that their idea of the proper path forward after high school had been trudged. However, I had no idea what I was doing there or what I wanted to do with a degree. My university days lasted a grand total of one full semester. I didn't pass any classes, but I had a great time! I lived in residence, attended very few classes, but a lot of parties. Of course, we never discussed the financial repercussions of my choices. I was in the dark about how much family money I actually spent (and wasted).

I came home, worked for a bit, and weighed my options. I even discussed getting into real estate in my early twenties, but my father talked me out of it. He told me it was for old people and retirees, and I would never make any money at it. He wanted me to have a job. The end goal was always a job. A steady paycheck delivered to my bank account on a predictable schedule by a business owner—a business owner who was not me.

My dad never shared in my optimism that I could make a career for myself independent from a corporation, which is interesting coming from someone who runs his own business and has been wildly successful for decades. Why neither of my parents thought I could become successful on my own, I may never know.

After I came home from university, my parents heavily encouraged me to pursue a diploma in some type of administrative field or childcare. This is where they thought my strengths were. I was a young woman, so what else could I possibly do, right? I ended up completing both programs, so I now have a diploma in Executive Administration and Early Childhood Education. Neither field has the potential to earn a living, but at least I have a piece of paper saying I am competent enough to answer a phone and keep a calendar. One day, should I so choose, I could go to a painstakingly tedious interview and plead my competency to a boomer who doesn't know how to rotate a PDF . . . all for the reward of a salary that might have been enough to pay rent in 1999.

I believe it was always my parents' expectations that I would marry a man who would be the breadwinner of the family. I do not fault them for having this expectation. This was the world they grew up in, therefore, the life they chose for themselves and their own family dynamic is a reflection of that upbringing. However, what they did not foresee was that the economy would change so drastically that double-income families would become the norm— and not by choice, but by necessity. I had no desire to live on a meager income until I got married, especially given the state of the economy.

Most millennials followed the rules of the game. We finished high school, completed a post-secondary degree program, and entered the workforce with the same fortitude as our parents. We followed the rules, but then the rules changed. And then, before we even had time to catch up, we were playing an entirely different game.

Young women are not conditioned to think about money on a large, long-term scale like men are. Although outdated, the mentality that men will be the primary financial provider for the family, and women will switch from using daddy's money to her husband's money, is still prevalent. Although those systems are still in place, there are no longer any legal roadblocks that prevent women from unraveling those myths. Neither of those narratives empowers women to become independently wealthy. It is time for a paradigm shift, and your road to riches begins now.

CHAPTER 2
STARTING OUT

So you want to be wealthy, and you want financial independence and freedom, but you don't know how to get
there. Let's talk about it. You need to ask yourself the hard
questions and set goals. What does wealth mean to you?

For me, being wealthy means living comfortably and
not breaking out into cold sweats every time I go to the
grocery store. I want my kids to play sports and I want to
go on family vacations.

Maybe your version of wealth looks similar to mine,
or maybe you want a yacht anchored off the cliffs of
Greece. Whatever your version of wealth looks like, you
need to start with goals. You need a long-term goal, which
will be property ownership. Your goal is to own your own
home or an investment property. To achieve your long-
term goal, you need to set a series of tangible short-term
goals. These are the stepping stones that pave your path
to success. If all you do is set your lofty long-term goal of
property ownership and neglect to forge the path, your

chances of success will diminish. It will seem like an insurmountable mountain to climb. If you only set the goal of owning a villa on the Amalfi Coast without a concrete plan on how to get there, you are sure to fail. Your short-term goals serve as the stepping stones you need to put in place to achieve your ultimate goal of property ownership.

Step one: open a savings account. You need a savings account where you do not have access to the funds through your debit card or online banking. Start your squirrel fund, and if all you can contribute in the beginning is loose change, then do it. Have the account open and readily available. This is the first step on your pathway to success.

Many people think they can simply save their money in their checking accounts. They question whether there is a genuine need for a separate account primarily for savings. The answer is yes, you absolutely need a savings account. First, a savings account is going to have a different accumulated interest structure than your checking account. It is generally higher, which means that the money placed into your savings account will generate more accrued interest than it would by simply sitting in your checking account.

Another reason for a separate account is accountability. Many people, myself included, treat a checking account as expendable. Money goes in and money comes out, emphasis on the money going out. I use my checking account to pay for all my business expenses, bills, loan payments, and consumables like groceries and gas. I have the expectation that the money in my checking account is readily accessible for spending. Personally, I need a separate account for savings, and it changes my mentality about what I have access to for spending. Psychologically, I know that the money put aside in my savings is more or less untouchable. It is not disposable income, and it is not funny money that I can use to buy a fifteen-foot inflatable Santa Claus for our front lawn in December.

Now let's talk about savings. Not once as a child, teenager, or young adult did I ever have a conversation with my parents about finances. Finances were an extremely taboo topic in my home. My parents had an old-school mentality when it came to finances. Money was private. Whether our family finances were tight or affluent, I was never privy to knowing any details. There was always the outward appearance that our family was comfortable financially, and I knew no differently. We never discussed finances, and if I asked, I was told outright that we do not talk about money in our home and it is private. Everything from how much lightbulbs cost to how mortgages work was very hush-hush. Not a single cell in my brain possessed any knowledge about financial security or longevity.

When I was sixteen years old, I got my first job life-guarding and teaching swimming lessons. It was my first taste of financial independence and working part time. I was making enough money to accumulate a meager amount of disposable income that I used to go to the movies with friends and shopping for new clothes. I kept part-time jobs as I worked my way through college and into adulthood. It wasn't until I was in my mid twenties that my parents had their first and only discussions with me about money. They told me to save money, repeatedly, but not how to do it.

What does saving mean, exactly? What am I saving for, and most importantly, save what? I had no foundation for financial literacy. After decades of spending money, I was expected to know how to save money and grow wealth without knowing anything about it or ever having heard finance-related terminology. I didn't know what a tax-free savings account was or what I would use it for. I didn't know what a registered retirement fund was or what it could be used for. I didn't know what options there were for saving money beyond a standard savings account with my bank, which was, of course, the same bank my parents used.

Interest rates on investments? You might as well have been speaking gibberish to me. I was at a point in my twenties, very much into adulthood, and I didn't know what I didn't know. Not only did I not know what all my savings or investment options were, I didn't even know enough to ask the right questions, or how to find the right people to ask. So, in case you are currently in the same position as I found myself in, let's get into it so you can become a financially literate queen.

As a young adult, I was primarily working in childcare, which was and still is a very underpaid and undervalued career. It was drilled into me relentlessly to save, save, save! In between rent, insurance, car payments, and a meager social life, I was finishing every month in the red. At times, I had a second part-time job to pull myself up just enough to break even.

If you ask anyone from our parents' generation how to save. Without a doubt, they'll tell you to cut back on what they deem to be luxuries. Now remember, the end goal is property ownership. So, if you are having trouble saving, you may need to make some concessions. I will explain a more effective cost-cutting strategy than forgoing what I would consider daily conveniences as opposed to luxury splurges. For argument's sake, I'm going to break down the cost of buying lunch every day.

Packing a lunch = $10.00/day

Buying a lunch = $20.00/day

By packing a lunch, you can save $50 a week, which equates to $2,600 a year. Let's say you do this religiously for ten years. You are a supersaver, and at the end of ten years, you've saved $26,000. After depriving yourself of a simple convenience for a decade, you still haven't amassed enough for a deposit on a new home, let alone a down payment or closing costs. *Whomp Whomp.*

The vast majority of our generation is crippled by the feeling of defeat. The media from older generations keeps shoving the narrative down our throats that young people need to make coffee at home and cut back on fast food. However, that narrative doesn't provide a realistic cost comparison to how or if this would actually impact our financial futures.

My mom likes to tell me a story about when she and my dad were first living together prior to having children. He was working full time, and she was going through grad school. Naturally, money was tight. Money was so tight that my dad called her one day and asked if she thought he could afford to buy a can of pop from the vending machine at his work. Even though my dad was the primary income earner at that time, my mom was still tasked with maintaining the family finances. She said no, he should not buy the can of pop, as they needed to save every penny. I heard this story dozens of times growing up, and I heard it time and time again when I was older and going through my lowest, feeling down and defeated about my personal finances.

My mom's perspective and intent on telling this story was to highlight the sacrifices my parents made to make ends meet and emphasize the hard times they put themselves through to get where they are today. My take on this story is that my parents had the luxury of surviving on a one-income household, and that money was just affluent enough that my mom could pursue a higher education without having to take on a second income for the home. On top of that, their story suggests that saving an extra dollar a day (or, at that time, maybe fifty cents a day) would make a tangible difference to their lifestyle and future wealth and success.

Which brings me to my next point. How your parents gained their wealth is not how you will gain yours. The rules that made your parents rich no longer apply. Simply having a stable, well-paying job is not enough to buy a house anymore. Demand for property is high and supply is low, which led to the housing crisis plaguing North America.

Depriving yourself of a $15 takeout pizza on a Friday night instead of going to the store and spending $40 to buy all the ingredients to make it at home is not sound financial advice. Our parents are well-meaning, but more often than not, they are completely out of touch with the current economy, and they can pry my meatlover's double cheese pizza out of my cold, dead hands.

If you have a savings account and a well-paying job that helps you make ends meet, you are well on your way to joining the ranks of home ownership. What you need now is a side hustle. Not a second job, a true side hustle. You will never gain true wealth or financial independence by working for someone else. It must be something you like, and it must be something you can make money doing. The idea is to turn a passion into a profit without burning yourself out. Fill your soul while also filling your bank account.

You are already maintaining a lifestyle with your nine-to-five job, which means every penny of profit from your side hustle goes directly into the savings account. The possibilities are endless. Are you handy? Flip furniture. Artistic? Sell your work online or at local handmade markets. Do you like baking or cooking? Hit up local mom groups and target your demographic who is planning the family meals and kids parties. Or turn your favorite recipes into a cookbook or blog. Whatever you decide to do, and I cannot stress this enough—target women. Your advertising, marketing, and sales campaigns, however you decide to do it, need to target women directly and appeal to them. I don't care if you're selling men's deodorant or boxers. Target women.

Women of the households, whether they're wives, girlfriends, or mothers, are the organizers. We are the project managers, and we hold all the buying power for the family. Women are typically researching products and recognizing the individualized needs of each family member. We purchase products and services for ourselves, for our children, and for the men in our lives. Even if you are selling men's underwear, if your products are appealing to women, you instantly have the attention of the primary consumer in every home. Focus on low start-up and overhead costs and a big payout. When you start, time will be limited, and you will need the juice to be worth the squeeze.

We are the generation that fuels the gig economy. The gig economy, even a couple decades ago, was virtually unheard of. People had one full-time job, and that was enough. Now we have Uber, Task Rabbit, Instacart and so many other options for services that focus on alleviating the strain on the home, and, in turn, the women of the home.

People use these app-based gigs because they are convenient. Providing app-based services allows people to make extra money on their own time and on their own schedule. You may be surprised at how quickly your side gig becomes your largest income stream. A lot of people end up leaving their corporate wasteland in favor of running their very own small business.

Imagine your income no longer being capped at a 1 percent cost-of-living raise each year. Picture not having to listen to HR spewing about how appreciated you are as they feed you soggy pizza on the last Friday of the month after granting you the opportunity to pay two dollars to wear jeans that day.

Don't shy away from opportunities only because you've been conditioned to think you aren't deserving of them or because you feel embarrassed at the thought of becoming successful. Own your success, and soon, your own property.

CHAPTER 3
DON'T BE AFRAID

My first child was born in March 2020 . . . the same week shit hit the fan and the entire world shut down. I was a disaster of a first-time mom, full of postpartum hormones and anxiety over the state of the world at large. Childcare was non-existent and, at the time, I had no idea whether it would ever return to its prior state. I took an extended maternity leave and completed the program to become a licensed real estate agent. My goal was to pursue a career where I had the potential to be wildly successful financially while also being as present as I wanted to be for my family. I made my own hours so I could work as much or as little as I needed, and I was extremely grateful for the opportunity to do this.

I recognized a need and I did what I needed to do by making accommodations and concessions in my personal and professional life to meet them. That year, I must have been asked a thousand times what my plans were for childcare. Not my family's plan . . . *my* plan. I told everyone I was changing my career because childcare services were limited

and the future availability of such services was unpre-
dictable. My husband was very supportive, but we never
assumed or discussed him doing the same. I can guarantee
no one asked him what his plan for childcare was during
that unprecedented time.

Throughout history, there has been an unspoken
expectation that the woman of the household would fill
the void of the unmet domestic need. In the childcare
case, I filled that void. It was the best choice I could
have ever made for my family and my career, but while
carrying the domestic load and starting a new career
with a baby on my hip, at times, that choice cost me my
sanity.

I was terrified of what the future held. There were a
lot of not-so-silent whispers from family and friends. At
best, they didn't understand my career change. At worst,
they didn't think I could hack it. I lost friends after leaving my corporate wasteland job, whom I will probably
never get back. I had to justify my decision to change my
career over, and over, and over again to people who simply didn't understand why I was doing it.

My biggest regret was feeling like I needed to explain
my decision. I felt like I needed other people to understand what I was doing. What was more than that, I
wanted them to be happy and excited for me; however, I
eventually realized that that was never going to happen.
I eventually came to terms that the opinions of others

had no bearing on my future success. My need for understanding and acceptance only acted as a roadblock in my career trajectory. I was allowing others to influence what I knew in my heart to be right, and I knew I could absolutely do it, and do it successfully.

My one constant and unwavering supporter was my husband. Knowing he was on my side and understood the sacrifices I was making for our little family was all I needed to keep chugging along.

This chapter focuses on pushing the boundaries of your comfort zone and not being afraid of change. If you never change, then nothing will ever change.

A lot of noise around the state of the economy centers around housing costs and inflation. Groceries in 2024 cost more than a mortgage payment did in 2020. Daycare costs as much as college tuition. Older relatives constantly ask if we've started college funds for the kids, as we shell out $25,000 a year for daycare. The answer is unequivocally *no*.

At this point in our lives, a college fund is not the right financial move for our family. Just because the previous generation had the luxury of being able to spend decades saving for this potential expense does not obligate you to do the same. The financial economy differs from your parents' generation. Your financial decisions need to be different, too. They must reflect the current state of your family and the economy.

The boomer generation and the media have done a wonderful job of making young people feel defeated in their pursuit of property ownership. I implore you to break through the noise and not be afraid to think big. When I began my real estate journey, I was afraid of pushing past the criticism I knew I would receive. A large part of me felt embarrassed by the possibility that I could become super successful. What would people think of me if I became very wealthy? The public at large already had preconceived notions about Realtors, viewing them as slimy used-car salespeople.

The fact of the matter is that—yes, the economy sucks right now, but people are still buying and selling real estate. Housing is a human right, and regardless of the status of the economy, housing is still a basic need that everyone will strive to gain and maintain. Throughout every economic downturn in recent history, there are people who can still see the rainbow through the storm. They are the ones who end up becoming very, very wealthy.

Recessions make millionaires. Being able to work within the current economy intelligently will be your key to success. If you can work with the system instead of against it, you will have the opportunity to purchase real estate and make money from your investment. There is no "better" time to purchase. Everyone is always trying to beat the market and wait for the perfect time to make their move. The fact of the matter is that all types of markets have their peaks and pitfalls.

When interest rates are high, buyers will have more options available and bidding wars will be rare. The caveat is that their interest rates and monthly payments will temporarily be higher. If you wait for interest rates to come down, buyers will flood the market. Bidding wars and multiple offers pick up, and you'll find yourself in the thick of the rat race. Your home's purchase price will skyrocket as a result of the demand. At the end of the day, it all comes out in the wash. The best time to purchase real estate is as soon as you are financially prepared to do so.

I need you to make a vision board. This goes back to the small tangible goals you used as stepping stones on your journey to property ownership. It might sound stupid, but it has been proven that having a visual reminder of what your goals are makes them more attainable. If your large goal is to buy a condo on the beach, put it up there. If you have heart eyes for that yacht off the Amalfi coast, put it up there. Go through magazines or just print something that you can look at daily. Seeing what you are working toward each day will keep you focused and motivated. If you have a visual depiction of your goals in front of you to keep you on track, it is a proven fact that you are less likely to impulse shop and spend money frivolously. This will help you be mindful of your spending so you can adjust your habits. Witness your wealth grow as the dream property you once thought was unattainable slowly turns into your reality.

Let's focus for a moment on your small goals: your stepping stones. Having a vision board is great, but without a plan to arrive at your end goal, you will certainly fail. If you have a long-term goal of getting your beachfront condo in five years, then what do the next five years of progress look like for you?

How much money does your dream condo cost?

We would all like a $3-million penthouse on the beach, of course. Is this going to be the first property you buy? Absolutely not. I want you to think big, but also be realistic. Let's focus on a two-bedroom condo in a nice, safe neighborhood with a beautiful view of the beach. Where you are living, does this cost $500,000 or $1 million?

Depending on your location, there can be an enormous discrepancy in property pricing. Your first step is to do a little research and figure out a reasonable price range for the average condo in your area. You can do this yourself simply by looking at your local MLS website. Keep in mind that the listed price you see online does not reflect the sale price of those properties. The actual final closing price for the properties might be significantly lower or higher than the listed price.

Real estate agents employ different tactics when list-ing properties online. Prices are based on the state of the property and what their clients (the sellers) would like to do. One tactic is to list a property significantly lower than market value to create a frenzy and encourage bidding wars. Generally, listing a property below market value will generate multiple offers on the property and bring the final sale price up to market value.

Another tactic you may see is a property being listed above its market value. This affords the sellers room to nego-tiate, settle for a lower price, and still be within the limit of what they were comfortable selling their property for. Then, of course, you can come across a property listed at market value where the seller is happy to review reasonable offers that match their expectations. Whatever tactic the Realtor and seller employ, 99 percent of the time, all properties of comparable value will sell for comparable prices. The point I'm driving home is that a listing price does not reflect the market value or the sale price of a home. Some subscription-based websites allow you to see property sale prices, or you can ask a local Realtor to provide you with the information.

How much money do you need for a down payment?

Once you have an idea of what your condo will cost, you need to budget for a down payment. A down payment must be at least a certain percentage of the property's total value. Depending on where you live, this percentage point can vary. In some areas, depending on the price of the home, a down payment can amount to over 20 percent of the purchase price. If the price of the property is below a certain threshold, you might qualify for a down payment as low as 5 percent. In some areas, there are incentives for providing a higher down payment, such as avoiding the need for mortgage insurance. Speak with a local mortgage agent to see what programs are available in your area and which ones you qualify for.

Is your credit in good standing?

If you have credit card debt, student loans, car payments, or any other type of debt, you need to pay off as much as humanly possible over the next five years before applying for a mortgage. You do not need to be completely debt free, because that is not always realistic in today's economy. If you can demonstrate an established pattern of paying all your bills on time and without help, then you will be much more likely to qualify for the mortgage you need to purchase the property. You need to meet with a mortgage broker and display a strong debt-to-equity ratio (how much money you owe versus how much equity you have). If you have more debt than equity, your chances of qualifying for a mortgage loan are lower.

How much money do you need to set aside for closing costs?

Closing costs are frequently disregarded and rarely brought up in conversation. Any Realtor worth their salt will have a discussion with you about closing costs. These costs include the financial responsibilities you need to be prepared for in addition to your deposit and down payment. You will have lawyer fees, land transfer taxes, and moving costs, among other extra expenses. These expenses are just as important as any other piece of the pie. Do not spend every cent you have on your down payment and leave yourself without a contingency fund. I recommend reserving a minimum of $10,000 to cover all closing costs and unexpected home maintenance fees for the first few months of home ownership.

Government Grants and Incentives for First-Time Homebuyers

Depending on where you live, your federal or provincial government may have programs to assist with first-time home purchases. There are grants and incentive programs available, which are vastly underutilized. Again, I encourage you to do your diligence and understand what you are signing up for prior to beginning your house hunt. You will not want to hear this, but your first property will not be your dream property. To be honest, it's probably going to be a dump. If you are serious about growing your wealth, look for the worst house in the best neighborhood. Throw your ego and your dreams of an HGTV move-in ready home out the window. Overspending and being house poor is not the flex you think it is. This is short-term thinking, and you will not see a rapid increase in your investment by doing this. If the market changes suddenly, you may also find yourself stuck in a property that's worth less than what you owe on it. You must focus on value and what this initial investment property can do for your financial future. Your first property will be your means of growing your equity. It is a stepping stone to your beach-front condo. Land is a finite resource. There will never be more of it than there is right now. Historically, housing markets have always trended upwards over time, with a few dips and valleys along the way. Intelligently investing in real estate will grow your equity, and if done correctly, it will grow quickly. This is cold hard cash in your pocket.

CHAPTER 4
SPEAK UP AND ASK QUESTIONS

My first house was a dump. I bought it in 2017 when the market was crazy. I made a firm offer on a property with no conditions, took no time to complete any type of due diligence, and got seriously burned. As a young woman navigating the world of real estate for the first time, I turned to my father for advice. My parents had bought and sold a few homes prior to this, so they were well versed in the process . . . or so I thought.

I learned that just because someone has experience with buying and selling real estate does not necessarily mean they have any idea what they were doing or know how to safeguard their investment. I was completely overwhelmed and severely uneducated about the process. My father set me and my boyfriend at the time (now husband) up with a Realtor he had used in the past—another older male, and we went to look at precisely two places. We decided to make an offer on one and the Realtor sent documents via email for electronic signatures, and we were told we had bought a house. The Realtor did not go over the contracts with us at all. We did not know what the clauses meant, and we did not know what we were signing. The Realtor was looking for a quick and easy sale for a low-value home, and he was not interested in taking the time to make us feel comfortable or knowledgeable about our decision.

My dad and the Realtor left me hanging with so many unanswered questions. I don't blame my father for this at all and, looking back, I'm wondering if he thought this level of service was normal. I don't think he knew any differently, and he probably didn't know he was receiving poor service over and over again from this lazy old man. Looking back, I don't know whether my parents didn't feel like I deserved the time to have my questions answered, or if they truly didn't know the answers.

I asked the Realtor if we could get a home inspection. He responded with a firm no—that we didn't need one for a condo townhome. He advised us that the condo corporation covers all major expenses. WRONG. If you have the opportunity to get a property inspection, always get one. Even with a new build, there is never a downside to getting a property inspection. Not only will you become more knowledgeable about the property you are buying, but you will also learn about defects, large and small, which you may need to address in the future. You will also learn about any major defects of the home, such as a crack in the foundation that may need to be remediated prior to firming up the offer. If the defect is too large or will financially cripple you, you have the option to walk away from the deal and get your deposit back.

Also, for any condo property, what you need to do is have your Realtor include a condition with your offer to have a lawyer review the condo's status certificate prior to finalizing the sale. You need to know if the condo corporation has any pending lawsuits, or if there are any major repairs that will cause an increase in fees. There may be bylaws that prohibit pets or any other aspects that will impede your lifestyle or enjoyment of the property. You will also need to know if the condo corporation covers roof repairs, snow clearing, plumbing damage, and the list goes on. A condo's status certificate is hundreds of pages long. It is an extremely important document that will give the lawyer all the information they need to pass along to you before you decide to purchase. Owning property in a condominium community will affect your day-to-day life.

I asked our Realtor what a condo corporation was and what they did. His response was a flippant, "Oh, they don't really do anything. It won't really affect you." WRONG. In very simple terms, a condominium corporation is the legal entity that represents the collective interests of the unit owners. The corporation allows individuals to own property while sharing the cost of maintaining the common elements with the other unit owners through the collection of condominium fees. The condo corporation can also stipulate bylaws, which all unit owners must abide by. Some common bylaws regulate parking, prevent owners from renting out their units for short periods of time, and limit the number or size of pets that owners are allowed to have.

I asked our Realtor if we could take the night to think about our decision, and he advised against it. Granted, the real estate market was very competitive, and homes were selling quickly, so I recognized the importance of making a decision post haste. What I didn't know was that our Realtor would have been notified immediately if someone else placed an offer on the property. Or, if someone else had already made an offer, he would have been aware of it. Our Realtor did not disclose these facts, which caused us to believe that if we didn't place an offer immediately, someone else could buy the property before we even placed our offer.

Offers also include an irrevocable period, which is the period an offer remains active. There is always a time frame during which other interested parties are notified and given the opportunity to submit an offer if a second offer comes to the table. Of course, if our Realtor had taken the time to go over our offer, we would have known this. We should have been the ones telling the Realtor the terms and conditions of our offer, but I guess he made this up himself to suit his own needs. We could have taken the night to think about placing an offer while still having the peace of mind that the property would not sell without our knowledge. What the Realtor didn't want to lose was his shot at a commission if we changed our minds.

If someone gives you limited information and doesn't provide context, making your spidey senses start tingling, you need to remove yourself from the high-pressure situation. Take a step back and slow the process down. Ensure that you approach the largest financial investment of your life with a calm and focused mindset.

I asked the Realtor if he could explain the documents to me. He responded with an insinuation that it was riddled with wordy legal jargon, and that it's a standard offer that everyone uses. I need to make this very clear to everyone who is reading this: it is 100 percent illegal for your Realtor to not go over paperwork with you, top to bottom, word for word. You have the legal right to understand what you are signing, and you should feel comfortable doing so.

I prefer reviewing the real estate transaction documents with clients ahead of time. That way, if the market is competitive and we are on a time crunch, they remain confident about their decision and understand their legal rights. We can take our time going over what we need to add to the offer to safeguard their investment and examine the clauses that protect their interests. It takes a lot of the pressure off clients when they can take the information away and come back once they've had the time to review it. With no added pressure, I can go over their questions, concerns, or review areas for clarification.

I asked both my dad and our Realtor about setting extra money aside for the renovations the townhouse desperately needed. The Realtor said he has nothing to do with that, and my dad said we needed to figure that out after we moved in. This was a super lazy answer from the Realtor and my dad perhaps just didn't know. The Realtor's answer was indicative of his ignorance or apathy toward new homeowners, or he simply didn't care.

The government or mortgage agencies offer programs and incentives that provide homeowners with additional equity or rebates for renovations and improvements. If you are interested in a major home renovation but lack the upfront capital to do it, consider applying for a Purchase Plus Improvements Mortgage. This option enables you to include the purchase price of the home and renovation expenses into your mortgage. You make your monthly or biweekly mortgage payments, as always, which includes paying for the renovation loan.

By improving your home's energy efficiency, you can take advantage of several rebate choices that will result in significant long-term savings. While it may not be expected of a real estate agent to advise clients on government grants and incentives, a true professional will be well-versed in areas that could help their clients be as successful as possible. It is also just good business practice. Realtors are considered experts within their field and should have answers to these questions, should their clients ask. My Realtor's lack of interest and knowledge has been and continues to be a disappointment to me.

Do not be afraid to ask questions simply because you're worried someone else might not have the answers. I find that women often stay quiet in the pursuit of not making others feel uncomfortable. It's not your job to manage your Realtor's feelings. If they're uncomfortable because they don't know the answer to one of your questions, that is their personal responsibility to work through, not your burden to bear. Just because you receive a disappointing answer doesn't mean you shouldn't have asked the question. It means that you need to keep pursuing your answer until you are comfortable with the answer.

I have to assume my dad did not have the same experience with this Realtor in the past, or why would he have referred him to me? The level of care and professionalism was appalling, but as I didn't know any better at the time, and I lacked the confidence to advocate for a higher standard of care, and I signed the line as I was told to. Needless to say, that purchase was a big mistake. The experience taught me the importance of conducting thorough research and not solely relying on recommendations or presumed professionalism.

We stayed in that home for three years, used the limited disposable income we had to fix it up a little, and then got the hell out of Dodge. We purchased our second home using a young female Realtor I knew from high school, and whom I reached out to on my own. The experience we had with her was night and day, comparatively. In going through the documents end to end with us, she answered every question we had, whether it seemed menial to her or not. We were thrilled to complete a full property inspection, as per her recommendation. She was readily available for every phone call and text message we sent her, and she worked with a wonderful team of administrative and staging professionals to get us to the closing date. Seeing the way she worked with us and cared for her clients, even though we were selling a crummy low-value home, was what encouraged me to get into the real estate profession myself.

This agent staged our entire home and took the time to go through every single document with us in detail prior to having us sign anything. Amidst a pandemic, she helped us manage the process of showings when we had a four-month-old baby and a puppy. She was also successful in securing our new home for us by staying in constant communication with the listing agent, even though the sellers already accepted a conditional offer. The conditions fell though, and because our Realtor had fostered that relationship, she was the first phone call the listing agent made. We were able to submit our offer immediately. She was professional, poised, and best of all, she actually knew what the hell she was doing and treated us with respect. A novel concept to some.

CHAPTER 5
WHAT YOU NEED TO KNOW
AND WHO YOU NEED TO KNOW

If you are really looking for an investment and a way to rapidly increase your equity through property ownership, you need to look for the crappiest house in the best neighborhood. Purchasing a rundown, low-value home in an exquisite neighborhood will give you the best opportunity to grow your wealth. Through renovations, landscaping, and market-value increases, you will gain significantly more value than by purchasing a completely renovated home. Should you buy a completely updated home in a rundown neighborhood simply to match your price point, you will not see a return on your investment until the rest of the neighborhood catches up to your property value. You are now the threshold for the area and there is nothing you can do to increase your property value other than waiting for the market to increase, which is going to be a slow grind.

You also need to research different types of home ownership. Talk to your trusted Realtor and mortgage broker about rent-to-own options or vendor take-back mortgages. Consider partnering with an investor or taking on roommates to help pay your mortgage.

In all my years in real estate, I have worked with many young men in their twenties and thirties (yes, I am still considering thirties young—just let me have it!). Many of them have bought properties independent of a significant other. Young men are getting creative with types of ownership and financing, and they recognize the importance of getting into the housing market as early as possible. They are willing to take a hit on what they get in the short term in order to get what they want in the long term. Conversely, throughout my real estate career, I have never worked with a young woman who independently pursued property ownership without a significant other. Ladies, your path to happiness and a wonderful life will not be through a man. Your knight in shining armor will not be your husband, it will be money. True wealth, freedom, and independence will come from you.

Ladies, what on earth are you waiting for? I know you have good jobs, comparable if not better salaries than your male counterparts, and some capital saved. If men can make this work, then so can you. There is no reason to wait. Prices are only going up, and we all know salaries are not keeping up with the cost of living. The time to make your move is immediately before you get priced out of ever owning a home. Remember, the five-year goal is still that beachfront condo. Are these options perfect? Are they what you want in the long term? Probably not, but you need to recognize the importance of short-term sacrifice for long-term wealth and financial security. These methods help overcome entry barriers and reduce financial burden. Now, let's dig into some of these ownership options.

A rent-to-own agreement is a home-buying method where you enter into a contract with a property owner. When you rent their home, a portion of your monthly rent is credited toward the down payment of purchasing the home. Your rent credits accumulate, and after a specified period, you will have the option to buy the property outright from the homeowner.

Your rent-to-own contract will need to cover a few points including the lease term, rental price, home purchase price, percentage of "rent" going toward your down payment, possession date (when the title will be legally transferred to you), and expiry date. The contract will also include provisions for voiding the agreement if either party fails to meet their agreed-upon terms.

Now, don't let the shiny prospect of a rent-to-own option fool you. It comes with its share of liability as well. Your rent will be extremely high for the duration of your lease. You will essentially need to accumulate a full down payment in a very short period of time. The property owner is also taking on an enormous risk and assuming liability should the contract fall through. Again, this comes at a cost; however, if you can afford this option, it also comes with benefits. The purchase price of the property is agreed upon when you sign the contract. This means that if your contract is a five-year term, after five years you are purchasing the property at the price you agreed to pay five years earlier. At the end of those five years, you own your own property and already have five years of appreciated value built in. Even though you will pay very high rent for the duration of your lease, you need to make that short-term sacrifice for long term financial security.

A vendor take-back mortgage is a private mortgage between yourself and the homeowner. The homeowner extends a loan to you (the homebuyer) for a percentage of the home's sale price. Until the loan is paid off in full, the seller will retain some equity in the home equal to the loan amount. This is similar to a loan from the bank. As the loan diminishes, the seller's equity decreases in tandem until the buyer owns 100 percent of the property. The advantage of a vendor take-back mortgage is that you are not at the mercy of the big banks. With private lending, the interest rate, monthly payments, and amortization periods are all negotiable.

The next option is to partner with an investor. I love the idea of partnering with an investor. This option is ideal if you have worked hard and have some capital saved, but not quite enough for your down payment and closing costs. What you need is someone with a little extra dough to help you out. This is where an investor comes in. I see this a lot when family members want to help their kids or grandkids buy their first home.

If you have $20,000 saved and you need $30,000, consider the idea of pitching an investment deal to a family member who has some extra cash burning a hole in their wallet. This would be the same business model used if you were purchasing with a friend. If you both have $15,000 saved up, you can apply for a mortgage together. After five years, you can review the home's appreciated value. Going forward, your options are to continue with joint ownership, one party could buy the other out, or you both sell and cash in on the appreciated value of the home. With the third option, you both walk away with the funds to independently qualify for mortgages on your own homes.

In any of these ownership options, you can add a roommate. The obvious benefit to having a roommate is the additional revenue, which helps to make mortgage payments. If you are sharing common spaces such as the kitchen and bathroom, then no lease is required, and you will not be giving up any legal rights to your home. You have a lot more freedom as to how long someone can stay, or how much you can ask for rent. You will not be bound by the laws governing lease agreements.

My cousin got into the housing market when she was young, right out of college. She had one or two roommates for the first five years she owned her home, myself being one of them. After a few years, her significant other took the place of her roommates and they were able to upgrade to their forever home using the accumulated equity. They could purchase their forever home, a $1-million property in their preferred neighborhood, because other people had paid her mortgage for years, which was an extremely smart business move.

When it comes to housing, you can either pay someone else's mortgage or you can pay your own. Those are the only two options. Someone else will either take advantage of your capital and build their own equity, or you can build up your own. You need to get creative and figure out how to get into the housing market as quickly as possible. Even if you are currently living at home with your parents, still soaking up that rent-free lifestyle, buy a property whether it be a condo, house, or duplex, and rent it out entirely. Have someone else cover 100 percent of your mortgage and watch your equity grow. When you are ready to move out, you have the option to either move into that property or sell it and cash in on the accumulated value and purchase your second property. Explore your options, speak with mortgage brokers, Realtors, real estate investors, and real estate lawyers. Do your own research and make an intelligent investment.

A huge hurdle that women must overcome before taking the next step is accepting that you just don't know what you don't know. This was my experience when I purchased my first property. I didn't know the right people to speak to, the right questions to ask, or what I should have been looking for to protect myself and my investment. Before you reach out to industry professionals, you need to know the right questions to ask. I'm going to break down some touch points for you to get the conversation started.

REAL ESTATE AGENTS

Q: What do I need to have prepared prior to starting the home-buying process?

At the bare minimum, you need to have a pre-approval for financing from a mortgage lender. This will allow you to look at properties within your budget and taper your expectations. As much as you would like to look at $2-million properties, if you are pre-approved for only $750,000, then you're just going to waste everyone's time, including your own, and you will only set yourself up for disappointment. I also recommend having a wants and needs list ready. You want a swimming pool, but you need a home office. Know what home features will be, and which won't be, a deal breaker when you're searching for properties.

Q: What other professionals will you be working with from now until closing?

It's not just your real estate agent you will be working with. You need a trusted team of professionals who all work together to close your real estate deal. In addition to your own real estate agent, you will work closely with the seller's agent, your mortgage broker, a property appraiser, and your real estate lawyer. Optional professionals, depending on the type of purchase you are making, could include a property inspector, contractors, engineers, land surveyors, environmental specialists, and municipal planning authorities. Your real estate agent will serve as a project manager, coordinating the required services to safeguard your investment.

Q: What services do you offer your clients?

The answer to this question will vary drastically from agent to agent. Everyone runs their business a little differently. As an example, my basic services for buyers generally include a professional home cleaning prior to move-in, maintenance services, and moving kits. Clients can benefit from additional services, which are determined on a case-by-case basis, depending on their needs and the property they want to purchase. Once you decide to sell your home and begin working with a Realtor, the range of services they over expand to include marketing, staging, and advertising.

Q: What forms do Realtors use during the transaction process? Can you please go over them with me before I make an offer?

The forms will vary depending on the province or state you live in, but the primary document that Realtors use is the Agreement of Purchase and Sale. This is a long, wordy legal form that protects the interests of the buyers and sellers during the sales transaction. This is where you, as the buyer, add in your conditions. Examples of conditions include getting a property inspection, getting a property insurance quote, requesting that the sellers include the pool table in the sale, etc. I always try to go over the document with my clients prior to making an offer. That way, when we are ready to make an offer, we can focus our time on the details of the specific property and the due diligence needed to protect their interest in relation to the transaction.

Q: What are your expectations of me as a client?

This is not a common question, but such an important one. When entering into a working relationship, I always want to understand my client's expectations and communicate my own. I expect open and kind communication. Although stress levels often run high during real estate transactions, I will work for my client's best interest. I also make it clear from the start that my clients can expect me to be honest and upfront. My approach is not to simply tell them what they want to hear in order to close a deal. Even when what I have to say is not what my clients *want* to hear, I tell them if I believe it is something they *need* to hear. I will always provide clients with all the available information. What they choose to do with that information is up to them.

These questions are basic surface-level inquiries that any real estate agent worth their salt should be able to answer truthfully and without hesitation. When shopping around for a Realtor, your goal is to find someone you trust, who has your best interest at heart, and is invested in working with you. If they truly want you to be successful in your pursuit of property ownership, they will have the answers to all these questions, and they will be happy to take the time to have the conversation with you.

If you're getting the impression that the agent is annoyed when you ask questions, or if they don't seem to know the answers, this should raise major concerns. Thank them for their time and advise them that you will continue to interview other agents. It may be controversial, but I strongly encourage you to tell them this. A lot of real estate agents are lazy and don't want to waste their time having hour-long conversations when they could be showing houses. It's these agents who give the entire industry a poor reputation. If you are polite and respectfully candid with your rejection, it will elevate your confidence and the standard of care across the industry. You are making an enormous investment, so you need your voice to be heard. You must continue asking these questions until you find an agent who will happily take the time to tell you everything you need to know prior to signing a buyer's representation agreement.

MORTGAGE BROKERS
Q: What must I provide to get pre-approved financing?

At the very least, you will need to provide your mortgage broker with tax returns from previous years, notices of assessment, and proof of employment. They will also need to know what type of liabilities you are carrying and their amounts. This includes car loans, credit card debt, student loans, and more. They will use all this information and your debt-to-income ratio to determine what you can realistically afford, and your level of risk to the mortgage lender.

Q: What is the difference between variable and fixed-rate financing?

Fixed-rate financing means you will make the same monthly payments for the duration of your term. So, if you choose a five-year term, your mortgage payments will not go up or down, even when the base rate fluctuates. With a variable rate, your monthly payments will fluctuate according to the base rate. This means that your mortgage payments could go up or down each month. You need to work with a trusted broker who will go over these options and clarify the risks and benefits, and help you choose the option that aligns with your lifestyle and financial needs.

Q: What is a good credit score and what factors contribute to it?

Ranges may vary depending on the credit score model, but typically 800 is the best score you can get. This is an excellent credit rating, and lending institutions would consider you a very low risk. A score above 740 is considered very good, while anything below that may require a discussion with your lender on how to improve your credit rating.

Five major factors contribute to your score:

Payment History—Are you paying bills on time, or do you have a history of missed or late payments?

Credit Utilization—This is the percentage of available credit you are already using. If you have a credit card with a $10,000 limit and you consistently keep your utilization below $2,500, then you would have a credit utilization of 25 percent. A credit utilization below 35 percent is very good; however, maxing out your credit card each month is very bad.

Length of credit history—If you're new to the lending game, you may have a lower score, which is out of your control, but lenders want to see a consistent, responsible history that demonstrates how you handle your credit.

New Credit—Applying for more credit could reflect your credit score. Even if you are in a stable financial position, consistently applying for more credit could ding your rating.

Types of Credit—Holding different types of credit allows lenders to see how you manage a variety of accounts. This can include car loans, mortgages, lines of credit, student loans, etc. This does not mean having ten different credit cards.

Q: How long will it take to process my application, and how long is my pre-approval rate good for?

There is no blanket answer to this question. It depends on your lending institution, however; you will need to know how long it takes your lender so you can be prepared. Once you get your pre-approval, you can start looking for homes. Typically, a pre-approval takes only a few days, but it could take a couple of weeks, depending on the complexities of your financial situation. Big banks will usually honor your pre-approval rating for 60–90 days before re-evaluating, so for the love of god, don't do anything crazy within those 90 days. Do not quit your job, do not buy a G-Wagen, and do not lend $50,000 to your best friend from middle school who promises to pay you back in two weeks.

The same red flags are consistent across every industry professional. If they appear to be annoyed with your questions, don't have the answers, or try to push you to sign something without fully explaining what it is, you need to leave. You can get a mortgage from any broker or any bank. Your mortgage doesn't need to be with the same bank your parents have used for decades, and it doesn't need to be the one your dad recommended. It needs to be with a broker and financial institution that is going to serve your interests.

Have a long conversation and ask the hard questions. Remember that these professionals need your business, not the other way around. There are so many wonderful professionals out there who are eager to dedicate their time to make sure you feel confident and satisfied with your decisions.

Women often feel the overwhelming need to please people. We don't want to make anyone else feel uncomfortable, but it comes at the expense of our own comfort. We set ourselves on fire to keep others warm. Women are labeled as pushy, aggressive, and even called bitches if we question or push back in any capacity. The expectation is that we listen, do as we are told, smile, and sign on the line.

This is especially true for older men who lack experience working with women, particularly when young women challenge their authority. In my experience with older men—and this applies to men in my family and men I have worked with professionally—they have no emotional tools in place to have a respectful conversation with a woman who challenges their views. Instead of moving forward with the conversation with respect and poise, they often get frazzled or triggered, and more often than not, they shut the conversation down all together. In their minds, they've already labeled me as difficult and there is no path forward.

This is because, for most of their time on Earth, women have not felt comfortable or even safe challenging a man's opinion. Doing so would not only have been frowned upon, but dangerous as well. We have been conditioned to smile and keep quiet to safeguard the fragile male ego as well as our own well-being. It will be very intimidating and might even feel scary when you begin to assert yourself, but remember, they need your business. You don't need theirs.

You are in the driver's seat and it will be very satisfying to get the answers you deserve. If you feel uncomfortable going through this process with a male, then I encourage you to find a team of women. Women will often provide a much higher level of care than men because we still feel like we have something to prove. Fun fact: did you know that patients who have surgery performed by female surgeons have much better outcomes immediately after surgery and years later? Women care.

So, ask your questions and wait for your answers. Don't fill the air because the silence is awkward. When a mortgage broker cannot respond to your questions, their silence speaks for itself. It is not your responsibility to make sure they feel comfortable with the transaction, and remember "no" is a full sentence. If you need to get up and walk away, you do not owe them an explanation, and you are not obligated to repeat yourself until they are satisfied. If their vibes are off, go interview someone else.

The brokerage I used to work for would host training sessions called Coach's Corner. Our broker of record and the previous owner of the brokerage ran the sessions. One morning, I'm at Coach's Corner along with four other young female Realtors. I was the oldest of the group and the rest were in their late twenties. We were discussing listing appointments and contracts, and the older gentleman insisted we always bring contracts to the listing appointments. He advocated that we continuously keep pushing the contract in the seller's face and basically refuse to leave their home until they signed it. He was going on about this in a very pushy "salesie" way, hoping the sellers would feel awkward, crumble under the pressure, and just sign the contract.

Every single woman in that room was noticeably uncomfortable. First, I'm not bringing paper contracts to a listing appointment. I might as well ask the client to chip it in stone. It's archaic and inefficient. Second, the coach's entire approach was pressure based. He failed to showcase his value to the clients. He wasn't confident he would get the listing based on merit and simply providing the best service and beating the competition by being better at his job. His tactic of choice was to employ pressure.

I spoke up and said I would feel extremely uncomfortable being so pushy. I wouldn't want to work with clients who felt pressured to work with me instead of feeling confident that I was the best for the job because I gave them the time they deserved to make an informed decision. The coach asked me if he was coming across as pushy and I said yes. Everyone in the room grasped their pearls, shocked at my answer. It was clear that this was not the answer he expected, and then he talked in circles, not really knowing how to move forward from there.

The entire group of women went out to lunch after the training session and collectively had a good laugh over how completely useless this sales tactic was. Not only was it unprofessional, in our opinion, it was uncomfortable. On top of that, it was just bad for business. Women do not have the luxury of being labeled pushy or assertive. These are just polite codewords for being a bitch, and we recognized how detrimental this would be for our business. Women have to come with the facts, but we also have to be personable. We have to smile and be soft and kind. It doesn't take much to be considered a difficult woman. That's why there are so many of us.

Although he meant well, the advice coming from a man in his seventies was hopefully just a reflection of being out of touch with the realities of today's young women who want to succeed in the business. Women know what people are looking for and they know to play the part. As an older man, the coach was used to getting what he wanted by coercion. His expectation was that no one would challenge what he said. Women, on the other hand, are used to justifying and over-explaining every decision they make because they know they will be questioned and challenged. We must be prepared. I was steadfast in my "yes" answer, and then I just stopped talking. I did not fill the air to justify my response and I did not offer further context. Stand firm in your convictions and place the onus of justification on the party that's looking for your business.

The main takeaway from this chapter is to break through the noise and the feeling of defeat. Yes, housing prices are going up and wages aren't keeping up. The media talks about this to death. What the media doesn't discuss is creative ways to venture into property ownership. You will not build your wealth the same way your parents did, nor will you get into the housing market the same way they did. That doesn't mean that it can't be done. Take your lemons and build an empire.

Our parents' generation could buy a detached home with a decent bit of land on a single income. The rules of our parents' generation no longer apply, and although he means well, you need to stop taking financial advice from your father. Don't take financial advice from someone who doesn't know how to rotate a PDF and is likely to ask you if you balanced your checkbook. What you need is modern advice to excel in the modern market.

We are the first generation in history expected to be less affluent than our parents. A large part of this is due to the boomer generation hoarding wealth in land and real property. Then they have the audacity to be irritated when their grown children are still living in their basements. They offer the same advice that helped them buy a home forty years ago when a house cost ten bucks and their down payment was a dollar. What they fail to realize is that traditional generational turnover played a major role in their real estate success. Empty nesters are no longer downsizing, which leaves young families with no options to upgrade their homes. The trickle-down effect has begun to affect home values, resulting in prices starting at $700,000. Our parents' generation is made up of retired seniors who live in four-bedroom homes in good school districts, and they wonder why we aren't enjoying the same standard of living. They tell us just to pull ourselves up by our bootstraps. What the hell is a bootstrap?

Don't be scared to think big. Women are more hesitant to take risks professionally, personally, and financially, simply because that is not what is expected of us. It's uncommon for us to see women buck the status quo. We feel like we need to play it safe and be the voice of reason within our family units. To secure our children's future, we require a stable source of income.

There will always be excuses to not move forward, but remaining stagnant won't bring you any closer to waking up to the sound of rolling waves, or taking a morning walk and feeling the salty breeze in your hair. The time for our daughters to see us for the trailblazers we have always been is long overdue. Our daughters need to see us unapologetically making moves for ourselves and for them. I implore you to move forward in your pursuit of property ownership. Be a role model for the girls of the next generation by making smart, calculated risks to secure your own and your children's financial future. Our daughters are watching.

CHAPTER 6

CLOSING COSTS:
WHAT TO BE PREPARED FOR

While we discuss value, equity, and savings, it is as good a time as any to discuss the additional costs you will need to pay on top of your down payment. The lump sum of the down payment always gets the most airtime, as it is, by far, the largest chunk of cash you will need to have set aside when purchasing your first piece of real estate. You will incur other expenses, such as government-enforced taxes and invoices from professionals who help you along the way. This chapter breaks down costs versus value, and what you should expect in terms of additional savings to close your transaction.

First, when you talk to your financial advisor, ask them about your interest rate and how they will get paid from your loan. Generally, the interest you pay on a loan or mortgage is how financial institutions make their money. You will want to get a breakdown of how much of your payment is going to the bank and how much is going to your financial advisor. There is no such thing as a free lunch, and no one works for free. If you aren't sure how someone will get paid from your transaction, you need to ask so you understand the scope of the financial transaction and then shop the rate. I encourage you to reach out to a few people and institutions prior to locking into a commitment.

As a purchaser of real estate, many real estate agents will tell you not to worry about the brokerage compensation, as the sellers pay for it, which is not entirely true. The sellers often pay the brokerage compensations to their listing brokerage and the sellers' brokerage, but don't get duped into thinking that doesn't come from the money you pay them for the property. Brokerage compensation is worked into the total sale price of the home. The percentage brokerages get paid varies by region, but it's typically between 3.5 percent and 5 percent.

Paying a brokerage at the lower end of the spectrum allows them to post your property to the Multiple Listing Service websites, and then they wipe their hands clean of the process and wait for an offer to roll in. The full-service brokerages and Realtors will offer an extensive listing package to ensure the property sells for the best value. The services could include handyman repairs, professional photography, video and drone footage, prelist property inspections, professional cleaning, home staging and the biggest expense of all: marketing and advertising.

It might shock you to learn how many Realtors will not market or advertise your property at all. Do not be fooled into thinking that just because your Realtor posted your property to an MLS website that they are also marketing it appropriately. These are two completely different things and marketing can make all the difference between selling below market value after two months or selling above market value quickly.

Now, sometimes the state of the market will dictate the speed at which a property sells, but marketing plays a large role in your success. With real estate, as with anything else, you get what you pay for. If you have an agent working with you for a 1 percent brokerage commission, once you factor in brokerage fees, professional services, board fees, and insurance, they are more or less working for free. Someone who's working for free will not be invested in your real estate journey, and they'll often be so stressed about their own finances that they'd do anything to make a sale, whether it be in your best interest or not. Good work isn't cheap, and cheap work isn't good. I bring this up so you can make an informed decision. When it comes to your biggest financial investment ever, don't cut corners to save a buck or two. Unfortunately, many people do and those are the sob stories you read or hear about in the news. Your Realtor is legally obligated to have a conversation with you about brokerage compensation. It is crucial to comprehend the payment structure of every deal and offer you engage in.

If you have the opportunity, never skip out on a property inspection when looking to buy a home. Depending on where you live, or where the home is located, property inspections generally start around $500. You would not believe the number of clients I've had to talk into getting an inspection because they did not want to spend the money. If you're spending over $500,000 on a home, please, please, please do not skip the property inspection in favor of saving $500!

The buyer pays for the property inspection, and it's astounding how often people aren't prepared for this expense. Take this as your official public service announcement and add a few hundred dollars to your contingency fund. Having this extra money saved up brings peace of mind, ensuring that your purchase is a safe and wise investment. I only recommend clients to forgo property inspections if they are up against a dozen other offers. Buyers make their offers more enticing by removing all conditions. In a competitive market, and after thoroughly weighing the pros and cons, this is the sole occasion where I'll make an exception and advise a client to forgo the inspection.

I will also advise clients who choose not to get a home inspection to set aside a large chunk of change to cover the unforeseen issues that could arise within the first couple of years of homeownership. In 2021, the market was at peak anarchy. People were offering their life savings, their souls, and their first-born children just to sweeten the pot. It was the hunger games of house hunting. It was cause for celebration if I submitted an offer on behalf of my clients and discovered ours was only one of ten offers. I submitted offers when ours was one of sixty!

In a market like that, there was no option to get a home inspection. Buyers couldn't confirm their financing or insurance options for the house. Forgoing such conditions is obviously not in the best interest of buyers, but honestly, it isn't in the best interest of sellers either. As a seller, I'd rather work with a buyer who could demonstrate the financial ability to purchase my house. Unfortunately, through the chaos, a lot of people defaulted on their offers and got themselves into some really hot water.

Interest rates fluctuate, which is why they are called variables. What will never change is the price of your house. People who spent their life savings on homes in 2021 when interest rates were low now owe significantly more money than their homes are worth. The reality is, those who purchased high are only paying monthly interest on their loans and aren't even reducing the principal. I said it before, and I'll say it again: It always makes more sense to purchase a property when the asking price is low. Interest rates will inevitably fluctuate, but your purchase price will never change.

Another expense you must be prepared for is taxes. You didn't really think you could buy something without the government getting a piece of the pie, did you? Depending on where you live, taxes may vary. In Ontario, all buyers are subject to land transfer taxes. If you are a first-time homebuyer, you will qualify for a partial rebate. This is something you'll need to discuss with your real estate lawyer prior to closing. You'll see the rebate on the statement of adjustments, which your lawyer will go over with you.

As the title shows, the statement of adjustments includes the adjustments that are split between the buyer and seller upon closing. As an example, if the seller has already paid property taxes for the full year, they will receive a rebate and the buyer will resume paying taxes as of the possession date. This also goes for hydro bills, municipal service, etc.

Speaking of lawyers, yes, you will need to pay these guys as well. A good real estate lawyer is worth their weight in gold, and they will ensure that your transaction goes as smoothly as possible. Should you hit a bump in the road, they are often your second line of defense, following a phone call to your real estate agent, of course. Your real estate agent will always be your first line of defense for questions and concerns. Should the issue be outside their area of expertise, the agent will always point you toward the most appropriate professional on a case-by-case basis.

Depending on the type of property you are purchasing, you may need a well or septic inspection. You may want to get the electrical safety authority in for an inspection. There are all sorts of unique situations that can arise depending on the type of home you are buying and the area it's in. There are so many tools at your disposal to help make sure your investment is financially sound. I strongly encourage you to use all the expert advice you need in order to feel confident in your purchase. Remember, this is the largest financial investment you will ever make. There are appropriate times to save money and take the cheap way out, and there are times to pay for excellent service. When your life is quite literally on the line, that is no time to cheap out.

CHAPTER 7
DON'T BE STUPID

I'm going to get into all the stupid things you're doing with your money that are pulling you farther and farther away from moving into your beachfront condo.

When I was in my late teens and early twenties, I treated all my money as fun money. I had no responsibilities and no extravagant living expenses. What I did have was a thriving social life. It took precedence over most aspects of my life, and why shouldn't it have? I was living my best life, with no one relying on me or expecting anything of me. My paychecks would go into my checking account, but the money would be gone just as soon as the weekend hit.

I won't be a hypocrite and tell you not to go out and enjoy life because, honestly, the memories of being in my twenties are amazing and wild, and I have no regrets. All I ask is that you be conscious of how you spend your money. Make a needs and wants list. What do you *need* to do with your money and what do you *want* to do with it? You *need* to put a small portion of every paycheck into your savings account, and you *want* to go out with your friends on Friday nights. Both are important, so set a spending limit for your night out and stick to it. When I was twenty-five, did I *need* to buy a fifth round of Jägerbombs at 1:59 A.M.? Of course not. I *wanted* to. What I *needed* was a cab ride home and a Gatorade.

You *need* to pay your bills. You *need* gas money to get to work. You *need* to buy food. These are necessities and non-negotiables. The wants lie outside of the nine-to-five routine. They include the things that fill your cup and make you happy. Our society often looks for instant gratification—an immediate boost of serotonin that wanes just as quickly. Do you need a new shirt, a $10 drink from Starbucks, or new home decor? Or will you get long-term satisfaction by spending the same amount of money and taking your kids to the zoo, or spending no money at all and taking them to the beach or park?

You don't need a new designer handbag or a pair of red bottoms. If you're more concerned with the superficial appearance of wealth than actually being wealthy, then you need to readjust your goals. This is what I mean by being conscious of your spending. Stay away from impulse purchases that have no lasting power. Our generation feels the pressure of keeping up with the Joneses, and social media has been a catalyst for feeling inept or less than worthy. What social media doesn't tell you is that the Joneses are broke as a joke.

In today's society, women have learned to emphasize the importance of their outward appearance. This applies to our bodies and our homes. Historically, this is where society placed value on women. There was an inherent need for a woman to add value to how she presented her beauty and her home, because throughout human history, this was all they had and all they could control. The home was the woman's domain, and how she presented it was a reflection of the homemaker. You see your neighbors posting about their beautiful vacations and home renovations, but what they aren't posting is their credit rating or the fact they had to get a second mortgage to pay for the renovation. Social media is a highlight reel that pressures people into keeping up with a false reality. It is a fool's game.

Wealth creation is all about perspective, and your focus needs to be on your long-term goals. Once you see money accumulating in your savings account, the joy will become addictive. Because I'm old school, I have a daily planner—not a Google calendar. It's a book full of pages that I fill with my own handwriting.

Every day that I don't spend any money, I highlight the entire day in green. I love seeing several days strung together in green. It's unbelievably satisfying. Why do I use green? Because it's the color of money, of course. It has the same effect as the vision board—a small, tangible and highly visible way for me to stay on top of my goals. It keeps me on track and keeps me motivated.

To reach your goals, you need to create a structure focused on long-term success. You will need to make some short-term concessions, but if you can't commit to making short-term compromises for five years in order to ensure a lifetime of financial security, then nothing I say here is going to help you.

Let's dive right into the cold hard truth that you probably don't want to hear. You need to reduce your spending habits. I'm not talking about cutting back on groceries or other consumables like diapers and soap. I mean not filling your Amazon cart with trendy seasonal holiday decor so you can flex on Instagram, or your kid's tenth monster truck—because he's such a good boy!

We are a generation that is drowning in stuff. We have far too much *stuff* and nothing to show for it. This *spend* trend can be chalked up to the convenience of online shopping. We are the first generation to experience the convenience of purchasing anything in the world that we want, with the ability to have it delivered right to our doorstep within a day's time. It doesn't even feel like we're spending money because there's no true transaction taking place. It's far too easy to spend money, and it's mindless spending. There's no thought behind the spending because the transaction can happen in mere seconds. This has to change, and I'll tell you how it can be done.

THE STUPID SHIT YOU BUY ONLINE

If you want to get serious about saving money, I challenge you to buy everything you need for an entire month from a single store. Consider which store will have what you need, and assign a backup store in case the first one doesn't have what you're looking for. Then consider how much time you'll have to invest in getting those items home. You'll have to get in your car, drive, park, walk through the mall to get to the store, search through the aisles, potentially talk to a sales associate, stand in line to pay for your items, and drive back home. You're exchanging a task that takes 30 seconds to accomplish on Amazon for a time-consuming process that adds a physical and mental load.

If every purchase you made was less convenient than *click-click-pay*, would you still make it? I certainly wouldn't. If I had to go out and buy everything from a physical store, I'd purchase only a fraction of what I do online. Now, I'm not oblivious to the fact that online shopping has been life changing for rural communities that don't have stores that carry everything they need. I get that *actual* shopping isn't manageable for everything, but I would venture to guess that, for the vast majority of online shoppers, physical stores with the goods and services they need are within a half-hour drive.

When you remove the convenience of ordering online, you'll be shocked by how much money you save. Try it for one month and then compare your spending to the previous month. Put the difference directly into your savings account. Creating a simple barrier like this will encourage mindfulness and make you consider how badly you really need the items you considered purchasing online.

THE "PINK" TAX

Here we go, onto the next stupid way you waste money. I'm not going to beat around the bush. Being a woman is expensive! Women's haircuts cost five times more than men's cuts. It's surprising how much more women have to pay for shampoo, body wash, and razors when they're the exact same products packaged in different bottles. Then we have makeup, feminine hygiene products, and underwear, and don't even get me started on underwear! Why can my husband buy a five-pack of boxers for $30, and yet I have to pay that for a single pair of underwear made with a third of the fabric?

The list of products and services that are marked up for women versus men is endless. I've been taking my son to the same place to get his haircut since he was a year old. It's a little kiddie place where he can sit in an airplane or fire truck, watch Paw Patrol on an iPad, and hopefully get through his haircut without going nuclear. The cost for a kid's cut is about $25. The first few times I took him, I thought nothing of the price. They did a great job on his hair, and the child-friendly service was great. The first time my husband took him, he came home talking about how insanely expensive it was. It blew me away when he told me that his haircut, including a tip, totaled just $20. I had no idea a man's haircut could be so cheap, especially when I considered anything under $100 for a basic trim to be reasonable.

So, how can you save money on products when corporations are preying on women and counting on the fact that we will pay more to smell like a delicate flower blossoming in the spring rain? To start with, stop fueling the insanity. Buy regular bath and body products. Dare I even suggest purchasing your products from the men's section? Yes, the containers men's products come in will probably be gray and not as aesthetically pleasing, but you're getting the exact same product for a fraction of the cost.

Both men's and women's products come in unscented options, so you don't have to smell like wood chips and wolverines, unless of course you want to. So go ahead and live your best life. The same idea applies to razors, lotion, shampoo, and conditioner. When it comes to makeup, you obviously don't have the option to purchase from the men's section, but I would like you to honestly assess what you need and how often you need to use it. Makeup is insanely expensive and can easily cost you hundreds of dollars each month if you're using a ton of product every day.

On top of being terrible for your skin, people already know what you look like, so you don't need to drop $500 every month at Sephora just to go to the grocery store looking like it's your wedding day. A few basic items should go a long way and last a long time, even if you use them on a daily basis. This goes back to making short-term sacrifices to achieve your long-term goals. Keep reminding yourself that short-term does not mean for the rest of your life. If you're serious about getting into the housing market as quickly as possible, that also means saving money as quickly as possible. Reassess your lifestyle, figure out how you currently waste money, and make some adjustments. This will be the easiest way to save for that down payment.

THE ENDLESS MYRIAD OF SUBSCRIPTION SERVICES

Did you cut cable years ago to save money in favor of subscribing to Netflix when it was just eight dollars a month? And then you added Prime, and then Disney, and then HBO, and then Crave, and then Paramount, and then, and then, and then ... and now you're paying more in subscription services than you were for cable.

Yeah, me too. This used to be a great way to cut spending, but now nothing is offered on the same platform. All the best shows are split between several streaming services and now Netflix, the OG of streaming services, offers literally nothing but your kids' favorite show that you can't stream anywhere else.

Over the years, service providers have increased the cost of internet to offset the decline of cable-using households. Needless to say, the world of streaming services has become a disaster. I am anxiously waiting for the big players in the game to come together and offer some type of bundling package to basically bring us back to the days of cable where we pay one bill for all platforms. However, in the meantime, you can most likely cut down on monthly subscription spending. Like Amazon shopping, the worst part about subscriptions is that it's a quick and mindless enrollment process. In just ten seconds, you're set up for getting billed $15 a month for all eternity.

Figure out which cut of meat you really need and start trimming the fat. This applies to music and TV streaming, and all the other subscription services out there, which seem to include just about everything you can imagine these days.

THE ONE-WEEK RULE

Another way I hold myself accountable and control my spending is by following the one-week rule. If you want to buy something, wait a week before purchasing it. This eliminates impulse buying. At the end of that week, if you're still dead set on getting the item, then go ahead and buy it.

Sometimes I feel like I need something immediately for a specific reason, like a new pair of winter boots because it's suddenly freezing cold outside. But then I wear my boots from last year for a full week and decide that they're actually still in great shape and pretty comfy. By the time I arrived at that conclusion, my desire to buy a new pair had faded.

THE PAPER-TRAIL NECESSITY

If you're doing it, stop using cash. Do not use it for anything. Ever. There is no record of where your money went or how you spent it. You are not Walter White. A paper trail is essential for tracking your spending and ensuring accountability. At all times, you need to know where your money is going. And for the love of all things holy, do not sign up for store credit cards. They are predatory beasts, and the initial promotional offer you receive will never be worth the long-term debt you incur or the interest you have to pay.

THE HOLIDAY BLUES . . . AND REDS, AND GREENS, AND PURPLES, AND GOLDS . . .

Festive shopping is a trap. You do not need to replace your seasonal holiday decor every single holiday, every single year. Do you remember the nostalgic feeling you experienced as a kid when your mom brought out that same dusty box of Christmas ornaments? Didn't you love seeing her pull out the handprint reindeer you made when you were three? Did you feel the magic of the season every single year when the lights went up around the tree? You don't need to spend thousands of dollars each holiday to create special and lasting memories. You already have everything you need, and your kids feel the magic. I promise you.

These are all the little expenses that accumulate over time and have a massive impact on your finances. They're also opportunities to make additional deposits into your savings account. Now, there's one big, major, humongous way to save tons of money in a short time. This is going to have a greater impact if you are between the ages of twenty and thirty-five. It's controversial, but stay with me. Weddings.

CHAPTER 8

THE SENSE AND CENTS
OF SPECIAL EVENTS

Weddings have traditionally been the largest and most celebrated event in a young woman's life, yet they're rooted in transferring property between men. You guessed it—women were the property that fathers transferred to their daughters' new husbands. Cultures across the world have celebrated this exchange for thousands and thousands of years. Now, don't get me wrong, I love weddings. Dressing up, shedding a tear during the vows, taking advantage of the open bar, and inevitability witnessing an uncle drink away his ambitions and make an ass of himself on the dance floor. I love everything about weddings, except for the cost. The entire wedding industry has gotten out of hand, and it's done a stellar job of highlighting the extent of the pink tax. I am going to discuss other people's weddings, as well as your wedding, and how you can save money.

Attending someone else's wedding is a big deal, especially if it's to support a close friend or family member. First, there will be an engagement party, which requires a new dress and maybe matching shoes. You'll buy a gift and pay for transportation to and from the venue. Then you have the stag and doe where you donate your money to fund your friend's wedding because they can't afford it themselves. Then you have the bridal shower, which involves bringing another gift. I would also like to point out there is no male equivalent to the bridal shower. This is strictly a female tradition. Then you have the bachelor-ette party, which is often a weekend away that involves a hotel stay, restaurant meals, nights out on the town, transportation, special games, and events for the bride. So far, you've allotted four weekends and thousands of dollars, and probably took time off work and arranged childcare for several of these events ... and your friend still isn't married!

Then, of course, there's the main event. The wedding day. You buy another new dress and shoes to match, and book a hotel room for the night or transportation to and from the venue. Maybe you have to pay an overnight babysitter to stay with your adorable little party-poopers. You've now committed to attending five events and spending tens of thousands of your hard-earned dollars just so your friend can sign a piece of paper and continue living life exactly as they had been prior to the whole dog and pony show. It is excessive and unnecessary.

When I was in my twenties, several of my friends got married in one summer. If I had declined even a fraction of the invites and banked the cash I would have spent, I'd have saved enough for a down payment. It's a hard sacrifice to make, and I'm not tone deaf to the fact that, in many cultures, a lot of familial pressure comes with getting married. Weddings are still deeply rooted in tradition, so just be mindful of your goals and where your money is going.

If you have tens of thousands of dollars to support and fund other people's events, you have the money to invest in your own future. You have the money to get into the housing market and start building your own wealth. Your mom's friend's college roommate's daughter, who you haven't seen since you were twelve, will not miss you at her bridal shower. Politely declining an invitation to an event that isn't personally or financially feasible is perfectly all right, and I am giving you permission to do so. Do not people-please your way into financial ruin.

Now let's talk about *your* wedding. Not only will you have to arrange and fund all the previously mentioned events, should you choose to tie the knot, but you'll have the additional expense of paying for the big day itself. In our parents' generation, most people had their parents pay for the wedding, or a large portion of it. These days, it's becoming more and more frequent for people to pay for a portion, if not most of their wedding themselves, especially when people wait until they are older to get married. Regardless of who is floating the bill, most couples still spend upward of fifty to seventy grand on a one-day party.

Weddings are astronomically expensive. If you're planning your big day, and have the capital, either through familial gifts or your own finances, I encourage you to have a discussion with your future spouse about where you want to spend that money. Do you want to invest in your future or a party? What matters more to you: the wedding or the marriage? I can't tell you how many weddings I've been to that cost upwards of $50,000, and the bride and groom wake up the next day still living in the same crummy apartment they've been in since college.

In many cultures, it's a tradition for the father of the bride to pay for the wedding. If this is the case, I encourage you to have a discussion with your father about setting yourself up for financial security and independence—something every father wants for his daughter. Don't shy away from uncomfortable conversations when your livelihood quite literally depends on it. Discuss scaling back on the guest list, venue options, and allocating a portion of the wedding fund to property ownership. The goal of the day is to get married, and you don't need to spend the equivalent of your down payment on the beachfront condo to do so.

My husband and I eloped, just like we'd always planned. We knew it would ruffle some feathers, but we never bothered planning a wedding. In early 2020, we already had our son and were living life as a family in a jointly owned home. The only thing that distinguished us from a legally married couple was a piece of paper. At that time, when the pandemic regulations capped gatherings at ten people, we seized our opportunity to have the wedding we always wanted. We got married with only our parents in attendance, and my uncle, who was a minister, performed the ceremony in my parents' garden.

The best part about our day was that there was no stress over planning an elaborate celebration. The day was completely centered around our little family, and it cost us almost nothing. We had a single-tier cake made from a local bakery and I ordered my wedding dress on Amazon. My dad barbecued steaks for dinner while we all pitched in and helped with the mashed potatoes and veggies. We danced in the kitchen while drinking wine and finished the evening with a paddleboard in my parents' pond alongside a campfire. It was the perfect day for our little family, and even with the pandemic restrictions behind us, I wouldn't change a single thing.

Now that my spiel about the insanity of the wedding industry is over, another stupid thing you might not be doing if paying off debt. Do you have student loans? Credit card debt? Car payments? You need to focus on lowering and ultimately eliminating all debt. If you have a hefty savings account and a steady, high income, and are ready to purchase property, your debt will be like a roadblock unless you get it under control prior to your pre-approval process. If your debt-to-income ratio is not what it should be, then all your hard work will be for nothing. The feeling of defeat will most likely cause you to give up on your pursuit of property ownership. If your side hustle is turning a decent profit, pay down your debt as quickly as possible. Once you see bills disappear from your monthly budget, the additional funds go directly to your savings account.

Cars are a depreciating asset. Classic and collectible models aside, your vehicle will never be worth more than it was the day you drove it off the lot. Despite what the salesmen say, you do not need a new vehicle every two years. Falling for a "great" sales pitch, refinancing, and upgrading every couple of years will drive you further and further away from home ownership, and you'll have nothing to show for it but more debt.

Leasing a vehicle so you can forever pay a monthly bill is insanity. Buy a used vehicle that's reliable and known for its low maintenance costs and longevity, and drive it into the ground. When you finally pay your vehicle off in full, do not mistake this feat for a sign that you should now trade in and upgrade. No, this is your grace period where you get to celebrate not having a vehicle payment and enjoy more of the fruits of your labor. Bank the extra cash. It will add up quickly.

Similarly, you do not need to upgrade to the newest iPhone at every launch. You use your phone for texting, screening calls, taking pictures, and doom scrolling. There's nothing you can do with the newest model that you can't do with your current model. Embrace the vision of long-term prosperity over short-term gratification.

When money has been tight and then, suddenly, disposable income is abundant, a big problem I see is that people tend to treat themselves. They feel as if they've earned the right to because they've been working so hard. I used to be notorious for treating myself. I work hard, provide for my family, and I'm the default parent who tends to my children's physical, mental, and emotional needs. Damned right, I deserve a little something for myself every once in a while.

The problem was, I treated myself a lot, almost weekly, until treating myself became the norm and my home transformed into a mountain of worthless impulse purchases. I've spent more time decluttering and donating stuff than I ever did putting the items to use. Instead of indulging myself, I should have put the money into my savings account.

This is why it's crucial to have a vision board—a physical reminder of what you are working toward. You do not need a zucchini spiralizer. What you need is a home for your kids and generational wealth for your grandkids. It also turns out that zucchini noodles are gross and pasta is delicious.

Once you see your wealth growing in your bank account, saving will become your new addiction. Your home and your mind will be so much clearer without so much junk getting in the way.

I grew up in a home where, if I asked for something and justified my need for it, most of the time I got it. No one ever taught me the value of a dollar or how many hours of work it took to afford things like new clothes or dance classes. I was used to the construct of simply getting what I needed or wanted.

It's an unusual construct—the traditional nuclear family. The husband makes the money, but the wife manages the children and the home, and has the authority to make financial decisions and allocate funds. She pays the bills, registers the children for extracurricular activities, buys clothes and school supplies, plans birthday parties, and plays an array of fictional (yet very expensive) characters to ensure the children feel the magic of every holiday. So why are women not being taught about money when they're the ones expected to manage it?

I've worked with several young couples who were looking for their first home. In many cases, it was the woman who brought the down payment for the property and had the money saved up for closing costs, leaving her male counterpart to split the monthly mortgage payments. In other words, the man was able to chip in to cover the monthly expenses, but he never would have been able to buy a home if his female counterpart didn't provide the capital.

In every scenario, the woman is still seeking approval from her partner. She prioritizes his needs above her own, which often includes that she shell out the cash to buy his first home. Couples can make a mutual decision and respect each other's input, but it is disheartening to see young women looking for approval from their partners when they are the ones bringing the cheese. These days, women have money, power, and influence. What many of them lack is the confidence to act assertively because they fear displeasing their partners.

A few years ago, I worked with a young couple that was looking for their first home. Interest rates were low, housing prices had tapered off, and bidding wars and multiple offers were scarce. They had hit the sweet spot in the market, and I was so excited for them to begin their journey and to see them become successful.

Their fairy tale didn't end as romantically as I had hoped. Every single property we viewed met their needs, was in a neighborhood they liked, and was within their budget. Each time the woman said she was ready to move forward, the man would always say something to the tune of, "It's great. I just wish it was a hundred grand cheaper."

Well, of course you do! But that's not the way the world works. I wish my morning coffee cost fifty cents, but that doesn't make it so. On several occasions, I reminded him that their personal finances don't determine market value. I showed them the stats from previous sales to illustrate what a great time it was to buy a home.

They hummed and hawed their way right into renting their friend's basement and have been there ever since. They're now completely priced out of the market and may never have the opportunity to buy again. When your Realtor advises you that it's a great time to buy, and they have the receipts to back it up, I suggest you jump. Remember, it doesn't need to be your forever home. A good-enough-for-now home will do.

If you're purchasing a property with a partner, I want you to be respectful and choose one that you both feel good about and which suits your family's needs. What I don't want is for you to cater to his needs and wants above your own. Remember, he wouldn't be able to buy property if it weren't for you and your savings, and he'll be profiting from the appreciating equity that your investment brings.

The second he signs his name to the ownership papers, he'll immediately benefit from the hard-earned dollars you saved. You have every right to demand respect for your needs. His desire for a detached garage where he can build his man cave and escape from the home does not take precedence over a functional eat-in kitchen—the heart of the home where you'll prepare meals while helping the kids with their homework. Having him meet your needs does not mean you will neglect his, but it's important to see things from different perspectives.

If the thought of asserting yourself without sounding like a nagging bitch is overwhelming, here are some phrases to help you move forward with confidence.

"I hear what you're saying, but we need to find a home that meets our needs ahead of our wants."

"This is our first home, not our forever home. It doesn't need to be perfect, but it does need to be functional."

Both comments are respectful and keep the conversation on track with you in the driver's seat.

CHAPTER 9

BE CONFIDENT

The crux of why women aren't pursuing real estate independently is that they lack confidence. Millennial women don't feel confident or empowered to take this step on their own. The issue is complex, but I'm going to outline some simple factors that separate success from failure in the pursuit of property ownership. Most of them have to do with your mindset and motivation.

First, focus on pursuing additional revenue streams and working on your side hustle. You cannot do this if you commit to doom scrolling for hours each day. Watching other people chase success and wealth won't get you any closer to achieving financial independence and prosperity for yourself.

Social media is great for ideas, tutorials, and even little brain breaks, but don't waste hours tumbling down the rabbit hole and forgetting about your goals. Remember, social media is just a highlight reel. It doesn't resemble reality in the slightest. Stop focusing your efforts on *impressing* people. Instead, focus on being *impressive*. There's nothing more impressive than quietly and efficiently achieving and surpassing your goals, and then watching your wealth grow. Focus on your side hustle and bring some type of value to people who didn't even realize they needed some. Silently become so impressive that you'll be impossible to ignore.

I follow DIY tutorials on social media. I love seeing someone pick up an old piece of quirky furniture from the side of the road and then turn it into something modern and beautiful. My favorite part of watching those videos is when people brag about how much money they make. With a little sweat equity and some new hardware, a dresser that someone else was going to throw out on garbage-collection day is now worth $800. Now it's a one-of-a-kind custom piece. DIY projects are creative, fun, and best of all, incredibly lucrative.

If you aren't exactly a DIY queen, that's okay. That was just one example. Find something that works for you and fills your cup . . . and bank account. It takes more than just saving to become rich. In this economy, multiple revenue streams are the key to success and financial freedom. That's what you need to focus on outside of your nine-to-five job. Take a look at the top earners you know. I can almost guarantee none of them became wealthy through working for someone else or without having multiple sources of income. The key to success is in diversity and learning to pivot.

By learning to pivot, I mean in your personal, professional, and financial life. If something isn't serving you, learn to pivot and move in a different direction. You don't need to captain a sinking ship. The wealthiest people you know likely have a few things in common:

They work for themselves, which means they aren't fighting salary caps and payscales.

They have more than one source of income, which has always been the fast track to wealth, and always will be.

Having systems in place to ensure that your revenue streams run smoothly is imperative. You'll need to time block, prioritize, and when needed, delegate.

Our parents' generation ingrained in us that if we work hard and remain loyal, we'll be rewarded for our efforts. Unfortunately, as any young person knows, this could not be farther from the truth. In fact, many employers post office-job opportunities that advertise higher salaries for new hires than what they're paying seasoned employees. Statistically, people who job hop every two to three years significantly out earn those who stay loyal to one company and wait patiently for an opportunity for promotion within.

You don't have to stick with the same employer for 45 years just to retire and collect your ice cream cone and a pin like a kid at Chuck-E-Cheese before they boot your old ass out the door. Learn to pivot and move around to get the most you can out of employment.

Another interesting way to grow your equity is to purchase a small business. I'm talking *really* small. You might not have enough equity for a home, but you may have enough for a teeny, tiny business. If you do it correctly, owning a business can increase your earnings quickly and get you into home ownership faster. If you do your research and don't let your ego get the best of you, you can purchase a lucrative business for a small price. A business such as a laundromat is boring, low maintenance, and most of all, quite reliable. A self-serve car wash is also a great example. It's very low maintenance and provides a reasonably steady stream of income for providing water, soap, and a vacuum. You can check in daily, replenish supplies, and know it won't monopolize the majority of your time.

Now I want to talk about your day job, where you show up day in and day out to earn that reliable, soul-sucking paycheck and be the good little corporate stooge your employer expects you to be. You need to negotiate your salary. Before you break out into cold sweats, I'm going to give you the tools to do this successfully.

1. Compile a list of major successes you've spearheaded or completed independently over the last year.

2. Demonstrate how you've proven to be an efficient and effective employee and have been "rewarded" with more responsibility for no additional pay.

3. If the employer isn't compensating its employees at the current market rate, showcase what competitors are currently offering for similar roles.

In my experience, women often graciously accept the raises employers offer them instead of advocating for the raises they deserve, while their male counterparts successfully negotiate for themselves. No one will ever pay you more than you consider yourself to be worth, and let's face it, corporations are greedy monsters. You could be their best employee and they'll still pay you the lowest amount they can get away with.

Go to the meeting with your personal stats and recent accomplishments, present your salary expectations, and make your argument so compelling it will be difficult to ignore. I cannot emphasize enough how important it is to talk about your salary with your peers. Employee compensation is not a secret, nor is it confidential information. Keeping salaries under cloak and veil with the threat of punishment only benefits the corporation. The lack of transparency and demand for secrecy is a red flag and should cause you to question employer motives. If a company is open to wage discussions and transparent in its policies, there's no reason for the shroud of secrecy.

Do you recall the middle school days when you had to give an oral presentation in front of the class, and you practiced your speech at home over and over again out loud? You need to do this prior to your salary negotiation meeting. Be prepared, practice, level up your language skills, and boost your confidence before you present your case to the boss. If you cannot intelligently articulate why you deserve a raise, you'll only be doing yourself a disservice, and you'll have a steeper hill to climb than if you had exuded confidence with poise.

Allow yourself grace and practice politely saying, "I wasn't finished speaking," and "Please wait until my presentation is over. I have the answer to that coming up." Expect to be interrupted, keep your cool, and don't let it shake you. Address the interruption with confidence, assert yourself, and stay the course. Prove to them that you are integral to the company and, most of all, how you make them money. The employer doesn't care that you have great attendance or that you meet expectations quarterly. These are bare minimum requirements. You're expected to do these things in exchange for your paycheck. Go above and beyond, and outline what you do that makes them money. Hit them in the pocketbook if you want them to open it.

Now I'm going to hit you with an uncomfortable truth that you will not want to hear—No one owes you anything. The economy is shit, but it is what it is, and you work with what you have. For so long, I felt overwhelmed, like I wasn't where I was supposed to be at my age simply because I wasn't as successful as my parents were when they were my age. I recognize that times are different, the economy is different, gender roles are different, and our family dynamics are different. My life and career trajectory are allowed to be different, too. Looking at the past through rose-colored glasses and comparing it to the present was only hindering my progress. My skewed perception allowed feelings of defeat to creep in.

Focus on working with what you have in the present, build on top of that, and look only to the future. Your sunny future lies in your beachfront condo. So, what do you have and how do you build on it? You have savings, or as we like to call it in the business world, liquid capital. *Liquid* refers to money that you can physically hold and spend immediately. It's not a physical asset like real property, or capital in a stock, bond, or the crypto *du jou*r. It's physical, tangible cash in hand, evidence that your hard work and hustle paid off and you officially have capital! *Happy Dance*

Now you have cash, and with cash come options. Money equates to freedom. The first question you should ask yourself is: Do I have enough cash for a down payment, closing costs, moving expenses, and a contingency fund for my beachfront condo? If your answer is yes, then it's time to talk to your trusted mortgage broker and get pre-approved for your mortgage. You need to get pre-approved for financing before you start looking at properties. Your budget will determine the style, location, and size of properties you'll be looking at, and you need to limit your search parameters to the ones you can afford.

Once you receive confirmation of your pre-approval amount, it's time to contact your Realtor. When your Realtor knows your budget, and your wants and needs, they can compile information on neighborhoods and property types that suit you. When you look at public-facing MLS systems like Realtor.ca or Zillow.com, don't let the asking prices scare you. Your Realtor will assess the true market value versus what the sellers are asking for. Just because a seller is asking $1 million for their home doesn't make it worth $1 million.

Your Realtor can run stats and review closing prices on recently sold homes to assess real market value. They can set you up on email lists to notify you when a property that meets your criteria hits the market. Or, if you prefer a more personal approach, they can chat with you each day to keep you informed about what's currently available.

If you see anything that tickles your fancy, it's time to book a showing. Something that I like to tell my clients, whether they're buying or selling, is that their personal finances do not determine market value, and have no bearing on what a property will sell for. If your budget and pre-approval is $500,000, you have no business looking at $1-million properties that will sell for $1 million. Or, if you find your perfect dream property within your budget, and the current market value is $500,000, do not piss off the sellers or your Realtor by insisting on a lowball offer of $350,000.

Of course, negotiations allow for a bit of wiggle room. Sellers always want top dollar, and buyers always want the best deal on the market. Properties sell for market value 99.9 percent of the time, so play nice and make smart choices. You're much more likely to get a bit of a deal when you employ friendly and respectful negotiating tactics instead of lowballing and applying a take-it-or-leave-it stance. When representing the sellers, any agent worth their salt will tell their clients to leave it. As the old adage goes, you catch more flies with honey than vinegar.

If you haven't got enough cash to pursue your condo purchase, but you have got a good chunk of change, then the next question you need to ask yourself is: What am I going to do with it? Are you going to stay the course and maintain your trajectory with saving until you can comfortably get into your condo, or are you going to invest? As I mentioned previously, you can invest in a safe but lucrative business, like a laundromat or self-serve car wash, or you can invest in a property. You may never have seen yourself as a small-business owner, but sometimes you gotta risk it to get the biscuit. Fortune favors the bold. If you want to grow your wealth faster, focus on smart investing and saving.

You may not be able to afford your dream condo yet, but you can afford something. If you can afford any type

of real estate, I strongly encourage you to invest immediately. Getting into the market is a safe and quick way
to grow your wealth. You can buy a property and rent
out the entire unit. This allows you to turn a small profit
while someone else makes your monthly mortgage payments.

You could also live in the property and find a roommate to share costs and reduce your living expenses. This
would be a short-term way to increase your equity over
the course of a couple of years, and then you can sell the
property for a profit and upgrade to your beachfront
condo. Or, you can pull equity from that property and
use it as a down payment on your condo while the rental
property continues to generate revenue for years to come.
You could also partner with an investor to jump right into
your preferred condo. A joint venture allows you to split
the initial cost of the down payment and closing costs,
but keep in mind that you will also share the equity with
your partner.

Unfortunately, not everyone in your life will see your
vision, and as sad as it is to say, some of those people flat
out want you to fail. It could be that they're envious, or
maybe they don't feel you deserve to succeed. They may
think you're stupid and don't know what you're doing or
that you haven't worked hard enough for your achieve-
ments. I cannot stress enough how much their opinions
don't matter. Their negativity doesn't pay your bills.

My biggest regret in life is not telling more people to kick rocks, respectfully or otherwise. As a woman, I held my tongue far too often and let others tell me what I should or shouldn't do. I was under the impression that most of the people I surrounded myself with (friends, family, romantic partners) had my best interest at heart and would be happy to watch me succeed at whatever I had going on at the time. I was young and naïve, but now that I'm older and wiser, I know better.

Once, a family member told me that my happiness offended her. She saw my family, career, and sunny disposition, and this offended her. I was never as vocal as I could have been, or should have been, and I honestly don't think I get enough credit for that. Stay far away from toxic individuals who don't want to see you succeed, whether this be a romantic partner or your best frenemy.

When you're starting out, people will think you're delusional and dumb, and that what you're doing will never work. They won't understand what you're doing or why you're doing it. Just remember that what someone else thinks doesn't really matter. You don't need the approval of others to shine. Other people don't need to understand your goals. Having someone else understand your career trajectory or pursuit of property ownership doesn't impact your success.

You will get patronizing comments from older family members who say, "Oh, I saw your little business thing online, sweetheart." Defending your actions or motives for someone who's not invested in your success isn't worth your time or sanity. I like to respond to comments of the like with, "Oh, cool," or "That's nice." It acknowledges their comment but doesn't invite further discussion on the topic.

If someone approaches you and genuinely wants to learn about what you're doing and support you, go ahead and have an open discussion. When you have someone who celebrates your wins, it keeps you accountable and motivated to do even better. You don't need to justify your path to financial success to bootstrap boomers who tell you that you're lazy and entitled, especially when a portion of your paycheck funds their pension, which our generation will never see a cent of. Stay away from toxic people and stay the course.

If you're a mother, you undoubtedly receive comments about how working toward your success will affect the children *and* your home life. "Who will watch the kids while you're at work?" "Do you have enough time for your career and family?" Or you get quick quips about being a superhero and doing it all like, "Look at you go, girl!"

Women are expected to meet their children's physical, mental, and emotional needs, yet mothers are greeted with the side-eye and criticism when they actively provide the financial security that ensures those needs can be met. Mom-guilt hits me hard when I need to leave on a Sunday afternoon to work for a few hours. That obligation cuts into the time I have with my children after they've been in daycare most of the week. Even though I haven't worked a weekend in months, I still feel a pang of guilt over not being home, despite the fact that what I'm going out to do is equally important. I contribute to the lifestyle our family enjoys—a roof over our heads and bellies full of chicken nuggets.

Of course, the kids are safe at home with my husband and they're having a great time, but the mom-guilt hits just the same. The worst part about mom-guilt is that dad-guilt isn't even a term. I have never once heard a dad say he feels guilty for going to work every day. No one asks dads about their childcare arrangements or family-management plans for returning to work after a new baby is born. Society's expectation is that he'll go to work to provide for his family.

Women are expected to sacrifice everything for their families, including their own physical and mental health, and they're called superheroes for it. It's like pouring from an empty cup. Societal expectations of millennial women are not sustainable, and worse yet, our children recognize this as the norm. We're doing ourselves and future generations a disservice by allowing this to happen. The time to break the generational cycle has long passed. Are older generations going to understand your family dynamic? Absolutely not. Are you going to butt heads with your mother-in-law over parenting and family management choices? I expect so.

One of my favorite sayings is, "Unless you're offering to pay my bills, I don't need your input as to how I should live." You don't need the Cryptkeeper telling you to pound the pavement and get some face time in with the CEO of a Fortune 500 company, as if that will be your rags-to-riches moment.

I also love those comments from boomers who've spent the past forty years working menial jobs at the same company. If they have the roadmap to riches, why haven't they used it themselves? Once you assert yourself, the most wonderful thing will happen. You'll find yourself surrounded by people who love and support you and want to see you succeed. Ignore the noise and keep plugging away at your goals.

CHAPTER 10
BUDGETING FOR SUCCESS

Create a budget that captures the things you want to spend money on. Many people create their budgets by working backwards. They look at their bills and required payments and allocate their money accordingly. Whatever money they have left at the end of the month is their fun money.

What I want you to do is flip this around and create a budget that includes the things you want to do each month and how much each will cost. Include your monthly bills as well the fun things like brunch with bottomless mimosas and a family day at the fair.

If you allocate funds toward specific *wants* in your budget, it'll help you stay on track and take away the guilt associated with overspending and treating yourself. Your budget doesn't have to look like you paid an Excel professional to create it for you. Your budget tracker can be fairly rudimentary. It just has to make sense to *you*. See the following for an example:

Monthly Expenses: _____

Rent: _____

Car Payment: _____

Insurance: _____

Phone: _____

Utilities: _____

Groceries: _____

Student Loans: _____

New Boots for Kids: _____

Hockey Registration: _____

Brunch with the girls: _____

Fall Fair Saturday: _____

Savings/Investments: _____

Here, you have clearly laid out everything you *need* and *want* to spend your money on for the month. Your budget for each month will look different, and that's okay. This is real life, and you'll never have one month that looks exactly the same as the last month. The goal is to look ahead and predict how much money you'll need to set aside to make all your payments and meet your goals.

Fixed costs will often stay the same, but independent payments change each month according to your family's needs and the time of year. And, of course, you'll want to set aside some cash for yourself, too. Take away the stigma that mothers need to burn the candle at both ends and tend to everyone's needs but their own. Once you have your budget written out, keep it on your fridge or some place you can see it multiple times a day. Having it somewhere conspicuous will keep you accountable, like your vision board does.

While on the topic of creating budgets and making lists, I find that groceries are the one thing I constantly spend too much money on. You'll be more frugal and efficient if you make a shopping list and stick to it. Plan your meals and buy only what you need. When it comes to grocery shopping, the best money-saving advice anyone has ever given me is to allow things to run out. Let your home run out of cereal, milk, eggs, and snacks. You don't need a running supply of everything. Use what you have and allow yourself to run out of stock before buying more. You don't have to shop at bougie grocery stores either. Yeah, the lighting is nice, and the aesthetics are pleasing, but a can of soup is a can of soup, and you can save significantly by shopping at the lower frills stores.

One of the most important things you need to be conscious of while hustling and building your wealthy life is the threat of burnout. Take time for yourself and avoid it by keeping yourself mentally and physically healthy. If you focus only on grinding away and allocating every waking second to making money and improving your financial future, it'll catch up to you and you'll eventually collapse under the pressure.

You're allowed to enjoy life on your path to financial freedom. A healthy body and mind will elevate your success. If you're feeling overwhelmed, allow yourself some grace and shut down work for the day. Go for a walk, play with your kids, or have a dance party. Nothing will leave you feeling more refreshed and motivated than a much-needed boost of serotonin.

If you live with a significant other or children, I encourage you to get the whole family involved in the budget planning. Everyone needs to be a part of making the budget to understand its importance. If your children are older, it'll teach them accountability. They'll learn to take a proactive approach to planning their needs and wants for the upcoming month and be more understanding if they can't have the things they ask for in the middle of the month if those things weren't factored into the budget.

Realistically, anyone with kids knows they'll still ask for money well before the end of the month, but this will be a great opportunity to have a conversation about financial planning. You want your kids to grow up financially literate and comfortable discussing money management.

When I was growing up, money was a super taboo topic in my house. We never discussed money. Period. I didn't know how much money my parents made, or how much they were comfortable spending on us kids. I had no idea how much groceries cost, or what portion of their salaries my parents allocated to groceries, the mortgage, or family vacations. When I was a little kid, I remember asking my dad if you could buy a house with a credit card. His answer was "no."

I was old enough that he could have turned that question into a learning opportunity. We could have discussed mortgages and the various loans available from financial institutions, aside from credit cards, but the conversation ended there. What a missed opportunity.

As a result, managing finances was something I struggled with as a young adult. I drained my bank account on a regular basis because I didn't have the slightest clue how much money I should have spent on necessities. My ignorance left me overwhelmed and in overdraft. I can confidently say I've learned more about financial management from TikTok than I ever did from my parents, or during my entire K–12 education.

A trend that will send most boomer mothers into a tizzy is that most millennial couples, my husband and I included, do not have joint bank accounts—especially not savings accounts. Many couples now opt for a checking account for joint expenses and separate savings accounts. There's no need for a shared savings account in this day and age.

If you and your partner are both working full time, and bringing home equivalent or similar incomes, there's really no need to combine your savings unless you feel that's the right move for your family. However, when couples do this, it's often the woman who's tasked with paying all the bills, allocating funds for children's activities, and planning and organizing family outings. Once his money is in the bank, the man thinks his job is finished.

There's absolutely no reason for me to pay for my husband's phone bill and make his truck payments, or ensure that Netflix is paid on time so he can binge watch boring old war documentaries. Nor do I have any desire to save up for an ATV, but he does, so he plans and saves accordingly to achieve that goal for himself. He takes care of his finances and I take care of mine, and together we ensure joint expenses like our mortgage, utilities, and daycare get paid.

Please, do not add to your mental load by making sure your husband's car doesn't get repossessed. He is a grown-ass human and I promise he will figure it out, just as he had it figured out prior to you entering his life. Similarly, my husband has no desire to save up so I can go away for a long weekend with my girlfriends to wine country, but I do! And if I meet all my financial responsibilities, I can use my fun money however I see fit, and I don't need justification or anyone's permission.

Historically, sharing bank accounts has always been the norm, especially after a couple gets married. This only became the norm because it was illegal for women to have their own bank accounts, and a woman's only means of accessing money was through her husband, the gatekeeper to the cash.

My mother, who is in her seventies, clutches her pearls every time I mention that my husband and I have separate savings accounts because she cannot fathom why. Her perception is that this is merely a decision that benefited me because I'm a woman.

When my parents were young, my dad worked full-time hours to start his own business and my mother was going through grad school. It benefited my mother a lot to have access to my father's money, as that was the only source of income they had. When they had children, my mother worked part time. While she took time away from her career to raise us, my father's business became wildly successful, but only because he benefited from his wife's unpaid labor. She provided childcare, a clean home, hot meals every evening, and overall family–life management. He could focus on his company, unabated by having to stay home with sick children, sign school permission slips, plan birthday parties, or go grocery shopping.

My mother was the project manager of the family, but once my sister and I were older, she went back to working full time again. The dynamic of the home and task distribution never changed. My mother simply took on more. She could go back to work, but wasn't able to shirk her primary responsibilities at home. I never realized what it was when I was a child, but looking back now, I can only describe her presence as burnt out and, at times, checked out.

My husband and I are not in the same situation. First off, we started dating when we were both twenty-nine. We already had steady careers, and still do. At times, my income has been lower than his, especially when I took time off after having children, but when we're both working full time, we're pretty much even stevens.

Money ebbs and flows in every relationship. There's no upside for me to share a savings account with my husband, and I'd even argue that it would add to my mental workload. A shared account would eliminate my financial freedom and independence, and that isn't something I'm willing to give up without a good fight. I don't need to be responsible for paying my husband's phone bill, just as I don't expect him to take responsibility for paying mine. I find it interesting how many men expect women to take ownership of these responsibilities, but if the script were flipped, men would act like the ask was unthinkable. Women are not a never-ending free source of labor.

I would also argue that the primary advantage of keeping your own money in your own account is that you don't have to answer to anyone. You do not need to justify your purchases or spending habits. Your decisions don't require validation. You're growing your wealth through your own blood, sweat, and tears.

Do you really want someone asking why you bought a DQ ice cream cake last Tuesday when it wasn't anyone's birthday? Mind your own damn business.

WELCOME HOME

You've now successfully begged, borrowed, and stolen enough money to purchase a property. By working with your trusted mortgage broker, property inspectors, Realtor, and other industry professionals, you've found a property that meets your needs and budget, and is likely to appreciate in value. Now you're ready to make your offer.

Your offer is drafted on what's called the Agreement of Purchase and Sale, a long legal document that your Realtor will go over with you. Do not sign anything until you fully understand every section. The primary components you'll add to the offer include your offer price, deposit amount, closing date and, most importantly, any conditions (property inspection, financing, insurance, etc.). By adding conditions, you ensure that you complete your due diligence prior to the offer becoming legally binding.

Once your offer is firm, congratulations! You're officially a property owner! Well, almost. You'll take possession on closing day after the lawyers have transferred the title. After the title is transferred, you'll get a call to pick up your keys.

Then comes the moving day. Rally your friends, family members, and enemies. Bribe anyone you can with pizza and beer, and get to work. The physical task of moving can be a lot more than people expect. The one thing I hear more than anything else is, "How is it possible that I have so much stuff?"

Once you start packing and unpacking, you'll be shocked to realize how much stuff you actually have. Sort, donate, trash, and pack what's left. My advice to first-time homebuyers is to wait until after moving in to purchase furniture. I realize that you're excited to shop and furnish your new home, but give yourself some time to think about what you actually need and what furniture will be functional. Don't get ahead of yourself and order a sofa that you can't get through the door, or a bed you can't get up the stairs. Take a breath and slow down. There's no experience quite like celebrating move-in day with pizza and champagne on the floor.

Once you move into your new home, you'll begin making it your own. You can paint, change out the old linoleum flooring, and pull the shag carpet out of the bathroom. Little by little, the property will start to feel like your own as you transform the house into a home. Your property value will increase over time as you install upgrades and as the value of the neighborhood increases.

You've now successfully navigated what is often a very stressful experience with ease and poise. You asked all the right questions, and now you have your very own place to call home. No more slumlords or living in your parents' basement. You did it! Welcome home.

www.ingramcontent.com/pod-product-compliance
Lightning Source LLC
Chambersburg PA
CBHW071707210326
41597CB00017B/2375